The Costs
of Economic Liberalization
in Turkey

The Costs
of Economic Liberalization
in Turkey

Mehmet Odekon

Lehigh
University
Press

Bethlehem: Lehigh University Press

Associated University Presses
2010 Eastpark Boulevard
Cranbury, NJ 08512

The paper used in this publication meets the requirements of the American National Standard for Permanence of Paper for Printed Library Materials Z39.48-1984.

Library of Congress Cataloging-in-Publication Data

Odekon, Mehmet.
    The costs of economic liberalization in Turkey / Mehmet Odekon.
        p.   cm.
    Includes bibliographical references and index.
    ISBN 0-934223-75-0 (alk. paper)
        1. Turkey—Economic conditions—1960–   2. Turkey—Economic policy.   3. Monetary policy—Turkey.   I. Title.
    HC492.O25   2005
    330.9561—dc22   2004027848

PRINTED IN THE UNITED STATES OF AMERICA

This book is dedicated to my son,
Kerim Odekon,
whose infinite progressive enthusiasm
has always been a source of inspiration.

Contents

Figures

Tables

Acknowledgments

I thank Joy Fahrenkrog and Brian Anderson, my student assistants, for the computer support they provided. I am indebted to Jay Rogoff for his editorial help and Yahya Madra for his comments. Without Mary Crone's support the book would never have been completed. The project was partially supported by a Skidmore College Faculty Development Grant.

Introduction

WHY ANOTHER BOOK ON ECONOMIC LIBERALIZATION? AND WHY ON Turkey? The post–1980s era has been characterized by the triumph of the free market–based economic system. Politicians, the intelligentsia, the media, business leaders, and ordinary people alike have come to accept that a free-market economy is indisputably the most efficient, the most humane, the most socially and economically just, and, hence, the most desirable system. The collapse of the Soviet Union has provided the most tangible proof of the victory of free markets over regimes that regulate markets, leaving capitalism the unchallenged and undisputed survivor.

But like any economic system, a free-market system has several pitfalls that, unfortunately, have not received sufficient attention lately. Since economic liberalization programs prescribed for developing countries are predominantly based on the free-market system, a critical review of that system is long overdue.

A free-market economy serves only those producers and consumers who can afford to participate in the market at the factor and output prices set by supply and demand conditions. In other words, the "invisible hand" and the market equilibrium pay "rewards" only to consumers and/or producers who can afford the market-set prices. Free markets are predominantly concerned with allocative efficiency in the economy rather than with such issues as poverty, unequal distribution of income and wealth, environmental degradation, and the like. Any undesirable aspect of the free-market system is perceived as "temporary" or as a "short-run adjustment cost" and is assumed to disappear automatically in the long run.

Traditionally, the state and the government look after and protect the people. More precisely, the state supports those who could not or could only marginally participate in the free-market game, due to the fact that the market system rations out some producers and consumers at set prices. The roles of the state and government in contemporary free-market philosophy have been redefined in the "Third Way" argument developed by Anthony Giddens, a sociology professor and the director of the London School of Economics (Giddens 1998 and 2000, Petras 2000, Novak 1998, and Isaac 2001). The Third Way is embraced by self-proclaimed left-of-center politicians, such as England's prime minister Tony Blair, former US president Bill Clinton, and Germany's chancellor Gerhard Schroeder (for a critique see Barkan 2000). In the United States in the 1990s, the Third Way was reduced to the dictum, "workfare, not welfare" (notably similar to British "welfare-to-work" programs), and was the guiding principle in policy formation. The Third way claims that an active public sector in the economy is costly and inflationary, that the public sector is inefficient, and that the private sector can easily substitute for it. In the context of economic development, the public sector's inefficiency leads to deficits and consequently to an inflationary environment unconducive to investment, especially financial investment. Proponents of the Third Way, therefore, promote privatization and reductions in public expenditures to reduce budget deficits.

Unfortunately, the public fails to realize that a one dollar cut in the budget means one dollar's worth less public goods and services in the economy. Significant cuts in public programs, and increased privatization, have led to minimizing the role of the public sector in the economy, leaving the economically vulnerable groups without the protection of the public sector, and recently, to the mercy of the "invisible heart" (using Folbre's term [2001]), the cornerstone of the faith-based volunteerism in George W. Bush's "compassionate conservatism."

The negative income redistribution effects of budget deficit reduction in developing countries are reinforced by contractionary fiscal and monetary policies. These policies have typically had two goals: first, to reduce inflation, and second, to create an export surplus. Overall, it is impossible not to be reminded of Margaret Thatcher's and Ronald Reagan's supply-side economic policies of the 1980s. The difference, however, is that the promoters of these policies nowadays like to be branded left-of-center, whereas in the 1980s, they were labeled right-of-center.

A more drastic change regarding the economic role of the public sector is its repositioning itself from the demand side of the economy to the supply side, alongside the corporations. This redefinition of the role of the public sector in the economy is justified in terms of "employment creation." Presumably, the public sector's main responsibility in this new order is to ensure the enhancement of corporate productivity and profitability such that employment in the economy rises. Even in the Western economies, however, this employment creation has mostly occurred in the low-productivity and low-pay service sector, only affecting the published employment figures without significantly impacting poverty and income inequality. For instance, the US poverty rate in 1996 was still about the same as in 1986, 11.2 and 11.4 percent respectively (Economic Report of the President 2001, 314). On the other hand, rampant financial speculation and the internationalization of economic activity have contributed to a boom in incomes and wealth for the upper economic classes.

Surprisingly enough, the traditional critics of this kind of economic polarization in the West have been silent this time. The liberal intelligentsia over the last two decades has been divided into relatively small interest groups (for example, NGOs) focusing on ways to strengthen the socioeconomic status of their immediate constituency in the existing system. In other words, instead of questioning the fundamentals of the system and searching for viable alternatives, their time and energy are spent incorporating as many as possible into the system and thus strengthening the status quo. Whatever "left" there is is in shambles, trying to redefine "Marxism," "social democracy," and "left." The universities have been distracted from economic critiques because they have had to defend themselves against attacks from the political establishment and the corporate world and are busy trying to justify their existence and to readjust their finances and curricula to cope with the demands of the new high-tech era. The media have pretty much become a peon of the corporations, thanks to an ever-increasing dependency on corporate advertisement for survival but also as a result of the increasing concentration in the media industry. The public in general, and the working public in particular, now defend the corporate world because their livelihood and/or pension plans depend upon corporate success. Thanks to the silence of its traditional critics the corporate world has been capitalizing and expanding its economic and political influence in the West and elsewhere with little scrutiny. Globalization has become a corporate tool to exploit labor and natural resources in developing countries in the name of economic progress. This internationalization of economic activity, whereby the capital is owned by the Western megacompanies that use the cheap labor in developing countries and take advantage of their lax environmental and other regulatory laws, is seen as the only way to introduce sustained growth and development.

Obviously economic liberalization, imposed so forcefully on developing countries by the World Bank and IMF, has numerous fundamental shortcomings. Several of these are the subject of this book. Did economic liberalization increase saving and investment? What effects, if any, did it have on the environment? Has liberalization-led industrialization contributed to de-agriculturalization? What are the income distribution effects of these sectoral shifts? What have been the social, political, and cultural effects of economic liberalization? What are the human costs of liberalization? Are Western industrialized countries the sole winners in economic liberalization? Has liberalization contributed to a new kind of dependency? These are the issues this book focuses on. It is based on original research drawing on primary statistical and nonstatistical sources. It aims to contribute to the ongoing scholarly debate on the economic, social, and political effects of liberalization and stabilization policies sponsored by the IMF/World Bank.

Why, then, another book on Turkey? After all, Turkish experimentation with economic liberalization has been widely written about (Nas and Odekon 1988, 1992; Aricanli and Rodrik 1990; Kepenek and Yenturk 1994). Unfortunately most of these studies focus on the first decade of the liberalization program, from the early 1980s to early 1990s, and fail to provide a longer-term analysis. In addition, because of data limitations, they confine themselves to basic macroeconomic variables and to the external sector. Indeed, one important aspect of economic liberalization that makes it such a desirable development strategy is that its short-run impact on the economy looks positive. The macroeconomic performance in Turkey in 1980–86 was not an exception. The success of macroeconomic stabilization and the liberalization of the external sector have led Turkey to gain exemplary status in the IMF, World Bank, and OECD circles. What the international organizations failed to recognize, however, was that the liberalization policies, by increasing income inequality and polarization, were at the same time strengthening the religious movements in Turkey with significant social consequences. Islam emphasizes social and economic justice. The worsening distribution of income in the post–1980 era in Turkey provided the religious groups with the necessary ammunition for their rhetoric: Westernization concentrates wealth and income and contributes to economic and social inequality. On the other hand, the secular elite has seized on liberalization as a means of strengthening the Westernization process in Turkey, focusing on the political aspects of the latter rather than providing an economic rationale for its continued desirability.

This book criticizes economic liberalization within a simple dependency-oriented framework as a process that serves the Western industrial nations' economic, financial, and political interests instead of bringing Turkey and other developing countries widespread, long-lasting economic growth and development. These policies consistently favored capital over labor and created an economic system that made the rich richer and the poor poorer. If it has had any success, that success has been limited to the external sector. The cost has been increasing inequality and poverty, and the transformation of the structure of the economy to one that better serves the interests of the industrial countries. The first chapter will provide an overview of Turkey's economic liberalization since 1980. The next three chapters will contrast the myths of liberalization with its realities concerning financial liberalization, the agricultural sector, and the environment. The common theme of these three chapters is that economic liberalization creates an illusion of growth and development in developing countries, as shown in the case of Turkey. Specifically, the second chapter shows that financial liberalization has not contributed to a significant increase in saving and investment. The creation of the stock market and the introduction of new financial instruments have facilitated financial speculation and connected the Turkish economy to the global speculative network, but the domestic gains of financial liberalization have been limited. The third chapter argues that limited industrialization in Turkey has taken place at the expense of the agricultural sector. Turkey used to be a net food exporter, but today it has become a net food importer. Its agricultural sector has been reshaped according to the dictates of the international division of labor, whereby labor-intensive fruit and vegetable cultivation has replaced crop production in which the West and the United States have an advantage thanks to their technological superiority. De-agriculturalization has not only rendered Turkey dependent on food imports but also adversely affected the sectoral distribution of income in the economy. The fourth chapter focuses on the environmental effects of economic openness. The unprecedented rise in the exports of manufactured goods in Turkey has mainly originated in the so-called environmentally dirty industries. European industrial countries deliberately have limited the domestic production of such dirty goods and imported them, so the West has been exporting its high polluting industries to Turkey (and other developing countries), taking advantage of its lax environmental rules and regulations. The last chapter will critically review the relationship among economic liberalization, political and economic democracy, and human rights and will propose measures to strengthen labor's status in the contemporary world economic system.

The Costs
of Economic Liberalization
in Turkey

.

1

Economic Liberalization: Limited Success

In 1980, TURKEY LAUNCHED AN AGGRESSIVE ECONOMIC LIBERALIZATION program under the auspices of the World Bank and the IMF. Stabilization-cum-liberalization was probably the only viable alternative left for the authorities to cure the ills of an economy plagued by mounting foreign debt, foreign exchange shortages, high inflation, and unemployment. Economic and political instability were feeding each other, creating a vicious circle that threatened the country with chaos and bankruptcy. Under those conditions the authorities had little choice but to cling to the IMF/World Bank–sponsored stabilization program. The underlying assumptions of the program were that import-substitution-industrialization (ISI) had led the developing economies, including Turkey, to economic insolvency. Economic liberalization, based on the opening up of all the domestic and foreign sectors of the economy to the "superior" functioning of the free markets, would provide the necessary conditions for sustained growth and development. Only a few voices questioned the logic of this shift in development strategy. After all, South Korea, Japan, and other Asian tigers attested to the potential successes of economic liberalization. Only recently has the suitability of these examples been critically questioned and challenged (see, for example, Rodrik 1997, 1999).

This chapter starts with an overview of economic liberalization in Turkey, then focuses on the letters of intent signed by Turkish officials that describe to the IMF the details of the liberalization and stabilization policies Turkey would implement. The chapter concludes by analyzing the effects of the liberalization policies on the economy.

OVERVIEW

The theoretical foundations of Turkey's liberalization program are straightforward. The program is rooted in the neoliberal paradigm,

23

which argues that economic, social, and political development is best facilitated by economic growth. Growth is achieved by transforming developing countries' economies into Western-style free markets in a relatively short period of time. Only such a radical transformation would enable developing countries to access the private world financial markets to fund their development efforts. To this end, the first and foremost prerequisite is to remove all price and nonprice barriers to the free functioning of the input, output, and external markets. Eliminating these controls would ensure that resources in production would be reallocated in the economically most efficient way. Moreover, economic risk and uncertainty would be minimized by a commitment to low and controlled inflation. Since the government budget deficits cause increasing inflation, privatization is a concomitant aspect of the liberalization program. According to the neoliberal theory, the inefficient state economic enterprises are responsible for chronic large budget deficits, and hence inflation can only be lowered and controlled by privatizing these enterprises. In addition, privatization, along with deregulation, would increase competition, reinforcing the free market reforms.

Privatization, however, is not enough to control inflation. Stable monetary policy is as important. The continuous inflationary pressure in developing countries requires a contractionary monetary stance. An additional advantage of this contractionary policy stance is the creation of a domestic exportable surplus. The excess supply resulting from increased production and reduced consumption can be exported to obtain the foreign exchange necessary for intermediate and capital goods imports. The export industries are further supported by a significant real depreciation of the currency to eliminate the customary overvaluation. These core aspects of the liberalization program are supported by ambitious fiscal reform to generate revenues, by legal reform to support the provision and protection of property rights associated with the new emphasis on private ownership, and most importantly, by the liberalization and modernization of the financial markets, essential for the smooth functioning of the free market system.

The potential analytical effects of the program on the economy are captured in Figure 1.1. The initial supply schedule, S, is relatively steep to reflect the impact of structural rigidities on the price elasticity of supply. The effect of liberalization is captured by the new supply schedule, S', which has shifted down to the right and is relatively more price-elastic as a result of increased efficiency and competition.

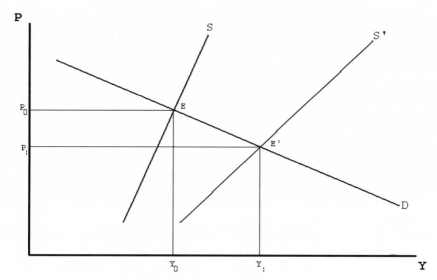

Figure 1.1. Effects of the Liberalization Program

Along the stable demand, the increased supply (S'), as a result of enhanced productive capacity, reduces inflation (price level decreases from P_0 to P_1) and raises production (output level increases from Y_0 to Y_1). On the other hand, the increase in efficiency enables producers to compete in world markets, meeting at least a portion of the foreign exchange needs.

The tectonic shifts this scenario causes has transitional adverse effects, that is, adjustment costs, which are considered temporary. The massive unemployment caused by stabilization, privatization, and structural changes have significant economic, social, and political costs. The 1999–2000 riots in the Philippines and other Asian countries, and those in Turkey in early 2001, are examples of such costs. The lack of any formal social welfare network aggravates the undesirable effects of liberalization on the economically disadvantaged and vulnerable. In addition, the increasing income and wealth gap exacerbates the frustration and unfulfilled expectations felt by the masses. Only in the new millennium, after decades of imposing one-size-fits-all liberalization programs, are the World Bank and the IMF beginning to consider their effects on income distribution and poverty in developing countries. Recently, the IMF has made several references to the need for having "social safety nets" to cushion the undesired distributional effects of the liberalization programs. (A chronological account of the IMF's social policy concerns is given in IMF 2000a.) Similarly, the World Bank (1995) has been emphasizing the importance of equity and equality in development and lately (March 2002) has even held a conference on the topic in Washington, DC. The IMF report explicitly recognizes that changes in relative prices brought about by the liberalization programs may have hurt certain groups, such as the urban poor, and admits, "a tension may emerge, therefore, between stabilization and social protection objectives" (2000a, 17). Furthermore the report argues that "the timely implementation of social safety nets has been hampered—all too frequently—by a lack of the existing social policy instruments. In addition to the lack of data, administrative and financial constraints have hampered implementation and monitoring" (2000a, 7). Thus references to the importance of the social safety nets still constitute only part of the policy formulation discussions and are not incorporated in the IMF conditionalities or other assessment criteria. Hence, it is still premature to agree with G. Nonneman's optimism: "The shift away from the 1980s-style neo-liberal policy prescriptions is well underway" (1996, 26).

The World Bank and IMF's overall neglect of the distributional effects of liberalization is not surprising. After all, these programs are simply an extension of the Washington Consensus (WC), based on the Thatcher and Reagan administrations' supply-side economic policies. The main features of the WC are deregulation, privatization of the public sector, tax reform, trade liberalization, financial liberalization, stable monetary policy, and fiscal discipline (Williamson 1997).

Like all supply side–oriented economic policies, WC reduces the cost of production and interest rates (especially the long-run real rates), which in turn raises profits, encourages investment, and stimulates growth. Eventually, WC claims, income growth would trickle down and benefit all groups in the economy. Unfortunately, this trickle-down historically has been limited. In most developing countries and in Turkey, the relative capital intensity in production necessary to reach economies of scale has restricted the labor absorption capacity in the manufacturing sector, leaving unemployment high and thus preventing any extensive trickling down.

Nevertheless, it is not a coincidence that the World Bank and the IMF are imposing on developing countries policies historically designed for industrial countries like the United States and the United Kingdom. After all, the decision-making power at these organizations is predominantly influenced by the industrial countries (for example, the United States is the main donor country to the IMF). It also seems developing countries lack viable alternatives and have no choice but to go along with the IMF/World Bank–sponsored liberalization program, even though there is no clear proof of such programs' success in fostering growth and development (for an extensive survey of relevant studies see Edwards 1993; Nonneman 1996). In the early 1990s, the World Bank (1990, 1991) claimed a strong empirical relationship between openness and economic growth, supporting the early pro-trade and liberalization arguments developed by Krueger (1980) and Balassa (1978). In the late 1980s Balassa (1989) championed once again the merits of outward orientation, and Dollar (1992) undertook a massive study of its impact on economic growth. Dollar's conclusion was that "the estimated gains of shifting to an Asian level of outward orientation and real exchange rate stability are increases of 1.5 percent points in Latin America's per capita growth and 2.1 percentage points in Africa's" (1992, 540). Eusufzai (1996) further argued that more open countries have higher, rising rates of improvement in human development.

Not all economists, however, agree with these findings. Even the IMF, as late as 1990, could not clearly support the view that its liberalization and adjustment programs had led to economic growth. In 1992, Woodward echoed the frustration of those critical of the World Bank and IMF policies: "Despite the relatively positive findings of the two World Bank studies on the issue, it also appears that structural adjustment has little or no positive impact on economic growth for the great majority of developing countries. On the basis of the analyses which have been carried out so far, there is no clear and incontrovertible evidence that structural adjustment helps to increase economic growth during the adjustment period" (1992, 96). Sinha (1995) supports this view in a study that shows that a positive outcome of stabilization and structural adjustment policies is neither analytically nor historically justifiable. Several free trade, openness, and liberalization skeptics would agree with this point (see Khan 1990; Khan and Knight 1985; Krugman 1987; Rodrik 1992; Doroodian 1993; Brecker and Choudhri 1994; Conway 1994; Pieper and Taylor 1998). The question then becomes why the IMF/World Bank promote liberalization so relentlessly. Do the liberalization programs aim at growth and development as ends in themselves or do they promote growth in the interests of the industrial world?

The case of Turkey is more interesting. As Table 1.1 shows, Turkish performance regarding growth and inflation has not been strong

Table 1.1. Growth and Inflation Performance: Developing Countries and Turkey

	Real GDP Growth Rate (%)	
	1983–1992	1993–2000
Developing Countries	4.7	5.6
Turkey	5.0	3.9
	CPI Inflation (%)	
	1983–1992	1993–2000
Developing Countries	46.9	21.3
Turkey	52.4	79.8

Source: IMF, *World Economic Outlook* (2001a).

and stable relative to the developing world as a whole. The average annual growth rate in the developing world has been 5.6 percent in the post-1993 period, whereas the Turkish growth rate was 3.9 percent. The inflation rate in Turkey has remained higher throughout the entire period and has soared since 1993. The average annual inflation rate in developing countries decreased in 1993–2000 to 21.3 percent, from 46.9 percent in 1983–92. In Turkey, inflation has leapt from 52.4 to 79.8 percent. However, Turkey's strategic location, its membership in NATO, and most importantly its potential as an export market all play an important role in securing IMF/World Bank loans. Turkey's real GDP growth in the last two decades averaged 4.5 percent a year (IMF 2001b). In 1995, approximately 80 percent of its population of 65 million people was younger than forty-four years of age (SIS 2000). Turkey is a large and young country with a per capita income of about $3,200 a year, an attractive potential market for multinational corporations. The growing capital market also provides an opportunity for multinationals to invest their profits as long as they are satisfied with the stable economic conditions. Developing countries in general have been a source of cheap labor, high profits, and speculative financial investment and export markets for the multinational corporations. The IMF/World Bank stabilization and liberalization programs appear to guarantee an economic environment in which the multinational corporations would feel at home to exploit labor, natural resources, and financial markets in developing countries. This kind of neoliberal globalization has made Friedman claim that we live in an economic age where "financial investors and multinational corporations [are] free from any nation state or power structure, and beholden to none" (Friedman 1999, 109).

Turkey joined the bandwagon of developing economies that experimented with economic liberalization beginning in 1980. First the military and then the civilian government committed themselves relentlessly to the IMF/World Bank–backed stabilization and liberalization programs. Plenty has been written about the Turkish experience with them (for example, see Nas and Odekon 1988; 1992; 1996; 1998, Dervis and Petri 1987; Krueger 1987; Krueger and Aktan 1992; Aricanli and Rodrik 1990, 1999). All these sources agree that in the first four years of the Ozal administration (1983–87), liberalization had somewhat succeeded, especially regarding the external sector. After 1987, however, the success faded, replaced by a series of crises continuing to the present day. Pieper and Taylor comment, "Through the late 1980s, Turkey was touted as an orthodox miracle. Now, in the wake of the financial crisis beginning in late 1993, it is a prime example of the BWI's [Bretton Woods Institutions] neglect of the potentially destabilizing effects of the changes in the income distribution implicit in their programs" (1998, 51).

Political instability has also contributed to economic failures. In the 1990s, first the Ciller (1993–96) government, and then the succeeding Yilmaz (1997–99) and Ecevit (1999–2002) governments were characterized by coalitions with different, sometimes irreconcilable political zeal and agendas, such as Ciller's secular, right-of-center and Islamic socialist coalition, or the social democrat and rightist/nationalist coalition that followed. Even though the reforms in the early 1980s have succeeded in separating the political and economic spheres from each other, political instability weakened the government's grip on the economy. Economic failures led to more than two dozen stabilization/structural adjustment programs with the IMF, which imposed conditionalities concerning sustainable current account deficit, fiscal deficit, domestic credit, and growth (Polak 1991, Krueger 1998). Specifically, the four main objectives of these conditionalities were to provide transparency to public policy, to assure the international financial markets of the government's commitment to macroeconomic stability, thereby minimizing risk and uncertainty, to assure the IMF that the government would pursue the suggested stabilization and liberalization programs, and to guarantee to the Turkish government that loan disbursements would be made as long as the conditionalities were met (Letter of Intent, December 9, 1999). Thus the aim of conditionality is to provide a market-oriented economic environment with price and exchange rate stability that would promote sustainable economic growth. Technically, the IMF extends credit to a country facing balance of payments problems under various different arrangements (for example, Stand-by Arrangements, Extended Fund Facility, Enhanced Structural Adjustment Facility or Structural Adjustment Facility) with different conditionalities and time horizons (see Polak 1991). Irrespective of the arrangement, however, the Fund expects the member countries to commit themselves to policies that would enable them to meet the policy targets referred to in the conditionalities. Interestingly enough, the Fund, which emphasizes transparency in member countries, has been reluctant to make these arrangements and conditionalities public until 1997–98. Krueger, who subsequently became the first deputy managing director of the Fund, comments, "This lack of transparency (which, at least to a degree, is surely necessary when issues such as exchange rate policy are discussed) has been the source of criticism of Fund (and, to a lesser degree, Bank) activities" (1998, 1985).

Initially, the focus of the Fund conditionalities imposed on Turkey primarily targeted exchange rate and price stability, and institutional reforms (for a detailed account see Krueger and Aktan 1992). In 1980, a crawling peg exchange rate regime (pegging Turkish lira against the US dollar with frequent adjustments) was adopted following a massive devaluation, and an ambitious export promotion program was put into place by liberalizing the import and export regimes. State Economic Enterprises' deficits were targeted for price stability, and legal and institutional reforms supported the export promotion policies. Still, the financial crisis of 1982 provided a brief setback. There is not much information available on the conditionalities of the standby arrangements until the late 1990s. It is still noteworthy, however, that the emphasis of the economic programs in the 1983–87 period has been different. Whereas the 1980–82 programs focused on inflation and current account deficits, the post–1983 policies evolved more around the free-market–oriented structural reforms and export promotion: "After 1983, almost all the changes introduced after Özal became prime minister focused on the structure of the economy and its outward orientation: government expenditures began rising again, and inflationary pressures were again felt in the economy" (Krueger and Aktan 1992, 51).

Several economists hailed Turkey's success with "openness." Kemal Dervis, a World Bank economist and vice president, who later in 2001 became Turkey's minister of state for economic affairs, was an outspoken member of this group: "Neo-classical two-gap models have given way to a focus on the efficiency and productivity associated with outward-oriented development. The case of Korea is an important part of the evidence on which the outward-oriented strategy rests. The case of Turkey, in turn, is beginning to provide a test of the theory. Here the outward-oriented paradigm was 'imported' into an unusually inward-oriented country facing a massive crisis. Turkey's dramatic policy changes in the 1980s were inspired by the conceptual framework of outward-oriented theory and come close to representing an experimental test of its usefulness" (Dervis and Petri 1987, 252).

The Özal government's policies contributed to rising inflation in the second half of the 1980s. In the interactions with IMF and World Bank in the latter part of the decade, the war against inflation and price stability once again became the focus of market-oriented structural adjustments. The unwillingness and/or inability to curb fiscal deficits, deteriorating external balance, and the Gulf War severely hurt the economy. The deterioration culminated in the 1994 financial crisis. The massive short-term capital outflow in early 1994 caused the value of the Turkish lira to plummet, increasing exchange rate volatility and interest rates. The April 5, 1994, standby arrangement included, among others, important policy measures such as 70 to 100 percent price increases for SEE products, a public sector wage freeze, massive cuts in public spending, tax increases to balance the budget, and structural reforms (OECD Economic Survey 1995, 26).

In spite of the fact that these measures boosted confidence into the financial system and stabilized the Turkish lira, the struggling economy could not get on its feet because of external shocks and continuing inflationary pressures. Even though the economy survived the 1997 Asian crisis, the 1998 Russian financial crisis and the massive 1999 earthquake in Turkey took their toll. In 2000, the continuing high actual inflation and inflationary expectations and the inability of the authorities to adjust the Turkish lira fully for inflation again caused large capital outflows, reducing drastically the foreign exchange reserves and adversely affecting the economy. The two most recent crises hit the economy in 2001. On February 19, 2001, a disagreement between Prime Minister Ecevit and newly elected President Sezer over power-sharing and corruption sent the financial markets into turmoil. In spite of the Central Bank's intervention, capital outflow amounted to US $ 1.5 billion. Overnight interest rates hit a record 2,000 percent, with a peak at 5,000 percent (IMF 2001c). It was obvious that the crawling peg could not be supported any more. Authorities decided to float the Turkish lira on February 22, 2001, and the currency depreciated sharply. Later in the year, the global economic and financial effects of the September 11 attacks were felt. The drop in foreign exchange receipts as a result of the global economic slow-down and the decrease in export and tourist receipts, as well as the decrease in short-term capital inflows, raised interest rates and depreciated the lira further. It seems that domestic and external factors continuously plague the Turkish economy, preventing it from settling on a stable and sustainable growth path. Unsurprisingly, Turkey has signed thirteen letters of intent (LoI) to secure standby arrangements with the IMF between September 1999 and June 2002.

The first six LoIs are distinctly different in emphasis from the last five. For instance, the September 29, 1999– January 30, 2001, LoIs focus directly on policies to promote growth and to reduce inflation. Structural adjustment policies, though still of primary importance, are not ends in themselves but means to achieve a stable economy. "Our policy objectives for 2000 and beyond are to achieve rapid disinflation, promote sustainable growth of output and employment, and strengthen the structure of the external capital account to reduce the economy's vulnerability. We intend to achieve these goals through a macroeconomic and structural adjustment program that could be supported by a stand-by arrangement from the Fund" (LoI, September 29, 1999, 5).

The opening line of the December 9, 1999, LoI voices very similar concerns and refers to the ambitious goal of freeing Turkey from inflation, enhancing the prospects for growth, and improving the standard of living for all (LoI, December 9, 1999, 2). According to the same letter of intent, the proposed disinflation program and strategy rested on three pillars: up-front fiscal adjustment, structural reform, and a firm exchange rate commitment supported by consistent incomes policies. To this end, the document first sets the performance criteria and the indicative targets for fiscal variables. Second, it describes an incomes policy that indexes the public sector wage increases to the targeted inflation rate with a provision to allow wages to catch up with actual inflation biannually if the actual inflation rate exceeds the targeted rate: "Salary increases for civil servants will be set in line with targeted CPI inflation (25 percent during 2000, of which 15 percent on January 1, and the remainder on July 1). We believe these increases will be sufficient to protect civil servants from erosion in their purchasing power. However, should CPI inflation during the first six months of 2000 exceed 15 percent, in July there will be an additional increase in civil servants' salaries equal to the difference between CPI inflation rate during the first six months and 15 percent" (LoI, December 9, 1999, 9). Actual CPI inflation in 2000 was 39 percent. According to the LoI, the public sector wages would keep up with inflation only if the CPI increase occurred in the first half of 2000. In this specific LoI, there was no provision for any wage adjustment for CPI increases in the second half of the year. In the December 18, 2000, LoI, however, the "forward-looking" indexation, indexing wage increases to targeted inflation, allowed wage adjustment in the second half of 2001 as well. Nevertheless, this catching-up process in the interim eroded the purchasing power of the wage bill.

The main advantages of the forward-indexing scheme are that it helps reduce inflationary inertia, sets the boundaries for wage negotiations, and helps keep the primary fiscal balances of state economic enterprises in check. It also increases the downward flexibility of real wages and theoretically increases the economy's ability to absorb adverse shocks. In its 2001 survey, OECD comments on this wage-setting scheme: "A notable gap in the programme has been that there is no effective institutional framework in place that would allow for forward-looking wage agreements to be struck in the private and state enterprise sectors and to assure an equitable distribution of the costs of disinflationary adjustment. Thus far, civil servants, minimum wage earners, and farmers have borne the brunt of the adjustment, as their incomes are subject to state influence and control" (OECD Economic Survey 2001, 17). The IMF, on the other hand, insists that this wage scheme is consistent with the fiscal targets and the disinflation efforts. It further recognizes the potential adverse effects of the disinflationary policies and expresses "intent" to minimize the unwanted effects on economically vulnerable groups by (1) reforming the public pension system, (2) legislating voluntary private pensions, and (3) introducing national unemployment insurance (LoI, May 3, 2001, 33). In the meantime, these short-run adjustment costs continue to be borne by the economically vulnerable groups. Recently, an Economic and Social Council has been legislated to allow the government to participate directly in wage negotiations in the private sector in order to moderate wage and price increases (IMF 2001c, 71).

Inflation targeting in the developing countries has been a relatively new policy strategy. Its success, to some extent, depends on the authorities' ability to forecast inflation, on their ability to fully understand the transmission mechanisms in the economy, and on the presence of a transparent and independent Central Bank totally shielded from fiscal policy influence. Moreover, macroeconomic stability, a fully developed financial system, and flexible exchange rate regimes are necessary for inflation targeting to succeed (IMF 2001a, 132). Even though the recent Turkish LoIs refer to inflation targeting as a policy instrument, in reality the Central Bank is currently targeting base money growth rate until the above-mentioned preconditions for inflation targeting are met (LoI, January 28, 2002, 6). Given the problems emerging markets have experienced with monetary targeting, which for all practical purposes the Turkish case is, the authorities may need to find ways to speed the adoption of explicit inflation targeting. The reason for the unfavorable experience of emerging markets with monetary targeting is "the instability of the relationship between monetary aggregates and inflation, aggravated by international capital mobility and financial liberalization" (IMF 2001a, 140). Furthermore, external factors also affect the control of the money supply. Changes in foreign interest rates and the resulting sudden changes in capital flows and currency substitution in developing countries affect the domestic money supply, rendering it difficult to control. Turkey has had its share in these destabilizing developments in the economy. Table 1.2 shows the extent of currency substitution and the volatility of short-term capital flows in 1990–2000. The widespread currency substitution, even though diminishing over time, and the sharp fluctuations in short-term capital flows do indeed undermine the stability of the relationship between monetary aggregates and fundamental macroeconomic variables, such as output and price levels.

Throughout the last two decades, policy authorities in Turkey routinely targeted fiscal deficits in order to eliminate high inflation and persistent inflationary inertia, uncertainty, and risk in the economy. It was hoped that a reduction in fiscal deficit would reduce the public sector borrowing requirement and would thus limit monetary growth and, subsequently, inflation. Figure 1.2 depicts the consolidated central government borrowing requirement (PSBR) as a percent of GNP and its growth rate. The relatively low level of the PSBR

Table 1.2. Currency Substitution and Short Term Capital Flows, 1990–2000

Currency Substitution (M2/M2Y)

1985–90	1991–95	1996–2000
0.798	0.612	0.55

Short Term Capital Flows (Millions US Dollars)

1990	1991	1992	1993	1994	1995
3000	–3020	1396	3054	–5127	3713

1996	1997	1998	1999	2000	
5945	1761	2601	759	4035	

Source: IMF, *World Economic Outlook* (2001a).

in the 1980s could not be sustained in the 1990s, especially after 1995. A closer look at the 1980s reveals that even then the authorities did not succeed at a sustained reduction in PSBR. A factor that has contributed to the post–1995 increase in consolidated budget deficit is the decline in the primary balance. The primary surplus of 3.3 percent of GNP in 1995 decreased to—2.0 percent in 1999 and later improved to only 2.3 percent in 2000 (OECD Economic Survey, various issues). Among the reasons for this disappointing fiscal performance were the usual suspects: State Economic Enterprises (SEEs), financial and nonfinancial. The fact that privatization and tax revenues

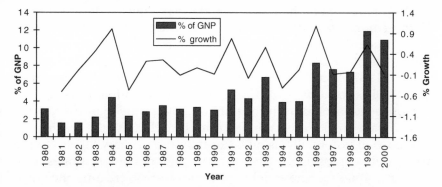

Figure 1.2. Consolidated Central Government Borrowing Requirement
Source: *OECD Economic Survey,* various issues.

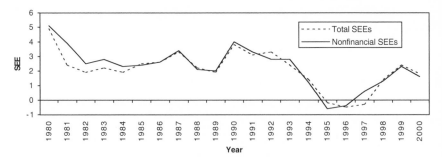

Figure 1.3. Public Section Borrowing Requirement: SEEs (% of GNP)
Source: Undersecreteriat of Treasury, *Treasury Statistics.*

consistently fell below projections only aggravated the fiscal balance. The borrowing requirement of total and nonfinancial SEEs is displayed in Figure 1.3. The sharp decline in the SEE deficits after the 1994 crisis has not been successfully sustained and deficits increased again as a result of the rise in the unpaid duty losses of state banks, notably Ziraat Bank and Halk Bank. Ziraat Bank provides subsidized credit to farmers and Halk Bank to small and medium size businesses. Thus they engage in quasifiscal activities on behalf of the Turkish Ministry of the Treasury. As a result of these activities, since 1993 they accumulated substantial deficits, which raised the total SEE deficits and PSBR (see OECD Economic Survey 1999, 57).

The fiscal deficit led not only to monetization and inflation but also to rising public sector debt. In 1990, the public sector debt reached 61 percent of GNP (LoI, January 28, 2002, Annex A). The only other time the debt/GNP ratio had reached this high a level was in 1987. However, in the meantime, there has been a significant shift in the composition of the financing of the public debt. More and more domestic borrowing replaced foreign borrowing, reducing the foreign debt to 18.3 percent of GNP in 2000 from 39.9 percent of GNP in 1987. Accordingly, the share of domestic debt has risen from 31 to 39.1 percent of GNP (IMF 2000b, 25). In addition, the increasing proportion of short-term public debt means that interest rate changes are quickly incorporated into the debt, with the real interest rate burden potentially rising faster than the primary surplus to prevent a debt explosion. Indeed, the very high real interest rates could trigger a situation where debt continues to rise, creating incentives for monetization of the debt (OECD Economic Survey 1999, 58). In this context, one should also consider the effects of financial liberalization on the cost of domestic borrowing. Rodrik (1992) rightly argues that financial liberalization has, on one hand, caused state banks to face ever-increasing revenue losses from competition in the financial market and, on the other hand, to face rising costs of borrowing because of increasing interest rates. Interest repayments to the net borrowing ratio in the consolidated public sector budget reached a record high 195.8 percent in 1995 and remained above 100 percent for the remainder of the decade (State Planning Organization 2002).

In sum, another important pillar of the World Bank/IMF programs has fallen short of its targeted success. The failure to reduce fiscal deficits, and slow progress in tax and social security reforms, privatization, and other structural overhauls have perpetuated the historical fiscal deficit-monetary expansion-inflation-slow growth axis in Turkey.

THE LETTERS OF INTENT

The letters of intent submitted to the IMF since 1980 discuss in detail the Turkish economy's proposed structural reforms. These reforms primarily focus on privatization of state economic enterprises, especially in agriculture, petroleum, aviation, communications, and banking. In addition, social security reform, institutional reforms to increase transparency, and banking and tax reforms are repeatedly detailed at length in almost all of these letters. It is interesting to note that with the May 3, 2001 LoI, the emphasis shifts from inflation to structural reform, which becomes an end in itself. Whereas the May 3, 2001 LoI states that "growth, stability, and structural reform are mutually reinforcing goals" (LoI, 2001, May 3, 1), the strategy for overcoming the crisis later the same year relies "on strong structural reforms, prudent fiscal and monetary policies under a floating exchange rate regime, and an enhanced social dialogue" (LoI, 2001, June 26). Privatization, enhancing the role of the private sector in the economy, and institutional changes to increase transparency and accountability constitute the core of the structural reforms as before, but they now are imposed with a new ruthlessness.

Even though privatization in Turkey has followed a stop-and-go approach, it has been central to political life since 1984. The IMF/World Bank push for privatization originates in the argument that the sales revenues obtained will reduce the fiscal deficit and that the efficiency gains resulting from privatization will contribute to growth (Davis et al. 2000). In spite of the fact that the literature shows no convincing evidence that the private sector in developing countries is more efficient than the public sector, the IMF/World Bank position is that privatization is a concomitant part of any stabilization and liberalization program. The proponents of privatization have not yet successfully refuted Rodrik (1988), who raised serious questions concerning the economic gains of liberalization. For instance, he argued that revenues from the sales of public enterprises do not necessarily mean a net long-term increase in fiscal revenues, since the sale value of these enterprises would not exceed the discounted present value of their future profit stream (Rodrik 1988). One also could add to this argument the fact that the current improvements in the financial positions of the Turkish State Economic Enterprises (SEEs) derive from their increased efficiency, thanks to decreasing labor costs, caused either by falling real wages or the nonreplacement of retired employees.

Political contention caused privatization to proceed slowly in Turkey. The opposing political and labor groups articulated successfully that privatization may lead to the control of strategic public enterprises by foreign capital. As a matter of fact, statism (that is, state capitalism) has been a basic tenet of Kemalism, the Turkish national ideology after 1923, the year the republic was founded, and a defining feature of Turkish economic culture. Just as Germans can be labeled as anti-inflationary or Americans as pro-business, Turks are for state economic enterprises, since historically the paternalistic state has played an important role in the culture. However, in spite of the political and to some extent popular opposition to privatization, a genuine effort to privatize the SEEs began in 1984. The state-run tourism bank (TURBAN) and the national airline (THY) were among the first SEEs to be privatized (for a detailed history see Ficici 2000; Karatas 1992; Kjellstrom 1990). Since then, various public companies have been sold to private ownership. These, however, were either small companies or ones in which the state held a relatively small share (Economist Intelligence Unit [EIU] 1999, 10). Nevertheless, in 1998, privatization revenues rose to $2.1 billion from $465 million in 1997 (EUI 1999, 11). So far, privatization has mostly taken the form of block sales to domestic and/or foreign private companies, thus failing to realize one of its main objectives: widespread share ownership in the economy (Karatas 1992; Keller et al. 1994). In addition, in some cases, as a result of keeping the regulatory framework intact, privatization meant the transfer of monopoly power from the state to the private sector.

By the beginning of 2002, important achievements in privatization had been accomplished. In addition to getting ready to sell the SEEs for which the technical preparations have been completed, notably TUPRATM (petroleum refinery) and POATM (petroleum distribution), the authorities committed themselves to completing in 2002 all preparatory work for the privatization of Turk Telekom (communications), TEKEL (tobacco and spirits), TSEKER (sugar), THY (airlines), ERDEMIR (steel), EUATM (electricity generation), TEDATM (electricity distribution), BOTATM (natural gas), and state-owned land (LoI, January 28, 2002, 13). To some extent, the renewed push for privatization is the result of IMF's concern with the slippage in the implementation of the privatization program, as detailed in letters of intent sent to the Fund prior to 2001. Hence the firm commitment in the January 2002, LoI to privatization, as well as to making Turkey "substantially" more attractive for foreign investment. Actually the January 2002 letter of intent goes as far as pledging the establishment of an "investor council" consisting of prominent business representatives from Turkey and abroad (similar to Davos World Economic Forum). These efforts regarding the firm commitment of the authorities to pursue the IMF-backed structural reforms have apparently pleased the IMF extremely. On February 4, 2002, the Fund approved a $12 billion increase in its loan to Turkey, raising the total amount of loans under the current economic program to $31 billion and making Turkey its biggest beneficiary (IMF 2002). IMF managing director Koehler, referring to the loan, said, "Turkey must 'flawlessly' implement its economic plans if it is to succeed" (IMF 2002). If it does not, it may indeed go down the Argentine road with its high and increasing debt and economic problems.

The banking sector has also been on the center stage of reforms since the 1999 financial crisis, as the next chapter will discuss. The Bank Recapitalization Scheme approved in early 2002 has gained the firm support of the IMF (2002): "The government's new bank support scheme, the legislative aspects of which were passed by the Parliament yesterday [January10, 2002], is designed to help the remaining private banking system survive the current depressed state of the economy, while making bank owners fully liable for all losses the banks have incurred. The IMF supports this scheme as the least cost solution to deal with remaining banking sector weaknesses." A list of the important aspects of the banking reforms can be found in the January 28, 2002 LoI.

Historically, in spite of the high proportion of the young in the labor force, the pay-as-you-go scheme for social security proved unsustainable and contributed to the fiscal deficit. The social security reform of 2001 lessened the government's social security obligations by increasing the minimum retirement age and the ceiling on social security contributions, among other measures, all designed to reduce the projected social security deficit of 3 percent of GNP in 2000 (IMF 2000b, 28). Currently negotiations are continuing to draft legislation concerning the purchase of defined-contribution pension schemes that specify the contribution to be made by both, the employer and the employee (Sayan and Teksoz 2001).

THE EFFECTS OF LIBERALIZATION POLICIES

To assess the effects on the economy of the economic programs implemented in 1980–2000, we will focus on the same macroeconomic variables used in Edwards (2001). The three key macroeconomic indicators are output growth, inflation, and the current account–GNP ratio. Figure 1.4 graphs these variables. The real GNP growth immediately following the inception of the 1980 program was impressive. The recession of 1979–80 turned around quickly and by 1987, GNP growth reached 9.8 percent. The weakening of the economy started thereafter, and the deep recession of 1994 set in. A rapid and robust recovery in the next three years was not sustainable, and later in 1999 the recession repeated itself. In 2000, the economy rebounded again, only to experience a deep recession in 2001; the estimated GNP growth in 2001 was –8.5 percent (LoI, January 28, 2002, Appendix A). Similarly, success in controlling inflation has been a limited one. The cold-turkey approach to curbing inflation in the early 1980s brought the rise in the CPI from 110 percent down to 37 percent. In 1988 and 1994, the inflation rate again jumped. Since controlling inflation has been the ultimate goal of all stabilization programs, it is worth assessing the programs' success in this regard. Inflation targets set by the LoIs for 1998–2001 will be focused on since only for this time period do the LoIs provide consistent data. The June 26, 1998 LoI admits that past anti-inflationary programs have failed and claims that post-1998 programs will bring inflation under control in a systematic way to reduce WPI-inflation to single digits by the end of the

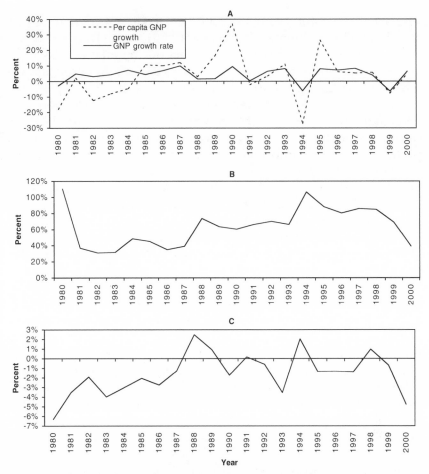

Figure 1.4 Change in Key Macroeconomic Targets, 1980–2000 (in %): Growth (A), CPI Inflation (B), and Current Account to GDP Ratio (C).
Source: State Institute of Statistics, various issues.

year 2000. To this end, the mid-1998 program sets the following inflation targets: 50 percent by the end of 1998, 20 percent by the end of 1999, and single digits by the end of 2000.

The actual inflation rate in 1998 hit 69.7 percent, about 50 percent higher than the targeted rate. In the December 9, 1999 LoI, the authorities revised the inflation targets: 50–55 percent by December 1999, 25 percent by December 2000, and 10–12 percent by December 2001. Again actual inflation remained above the targeted rates.

The actual rates for 1999 and 2000 were 68.8 and 39 percent, respectively. The preliminary estimate for 2001 was well above 65 percent. Unquestionably, significant reduction in inflation has been achieved in a short period of time. Nevertheless, domestic and external factors have prevented the realization of the targeted rates.

The improvement in the current account–GDP ratio is more permanent, even though the world recession, the Gulf War, the 1994 crisis, and the September 11 attacks all affected the current account and pushed it once again into deficit in 1999 and 2000. On the other hand, three debt indicators, the ratio of government deficit to GDP, the rate of growth of domestic credit, and the rate of growth of domestic credit to the public sector, reflect the extent of the government's compliance with the conditionalities imposed by the IMF (Figure 1.5).

Even in the early years of the 1980 stabilization program, deficit-GDP ratio exhibited a sharp increase. Subsequent moderation in the late 1980s was short-lived, and the deficit increased rapidly again in the 1990s. Growth in Central Bank credits to the government and in total domestic credit further provides an explanation for the persistent inflation in the economy. The explosion in the Central Bank credits in the early 1990s partially caused the 1994 crisis and the continuing inflationary expectations, affecting investment and growth adversely. Gazi Ercel, the former governor of the Central Bank, echoed these concerns in a speech: "Both the uncertainties stemming from high and volatile inflation rates and the increase in the costs of investments stemming from the higher interest rates and the devaluations reduced the incentives in the economy for the new investments" (1999, 6).

Since 1997, however, the Central Bank has virtually discontinued extending credit to the public sector, reducing total domestic credit expansion, which nevertheless still remained relatively high. By 1999, both the Central Government debt and total domestic credit were significantly above the World Bank's performance criteria figures. Thus the excess demand created by credit expansion has prevented the launching of an effective anti-inflationary policy.

Obviously the most successful aspect of the liberalization program has been the external sector, the result of a rational foreign exchange policy. In the 1980s, managed float of the Turkish lira kept it competitive enough to raise exports significantly, opening up the economy to foreign trade (Figures 1.6 and 1.7). In the 1990s, however, external factors again took their toll and the exchange rate appreciated, affecting exports and overall trade adversely. The 1994 economic cri-

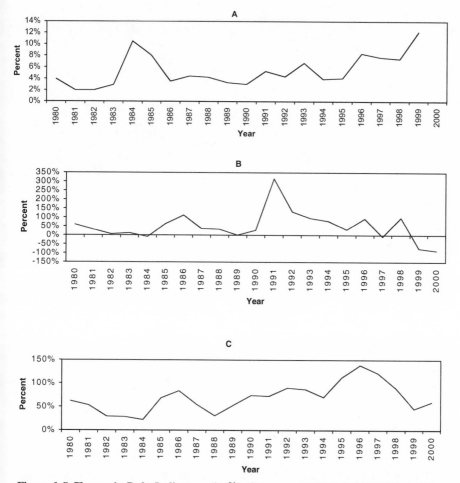

Figure 1.5 Change in Debt Indicators (in %): Government Deficit/ GDP Ratio (A), Central Bank Credits to Government (B), and Total Domestic Credit (C).
Source: State Institute of Statistics, various issues.

sis reduced imports drastically, pulling the current account–GNP ratio down. The recovery has been strong but short-lived.

An important aspect of the external developments was the change in the geographic distribution of Turkish foreign trade. The share of OECD countries in exports and imports increased steadily. The share of exports to OECD countries increased from 45 percent in early 1980s to 63 percent in 1998, and that of imports from OECD countries rose from 50 percent to 73 percent (OECD, various issues). Cor-

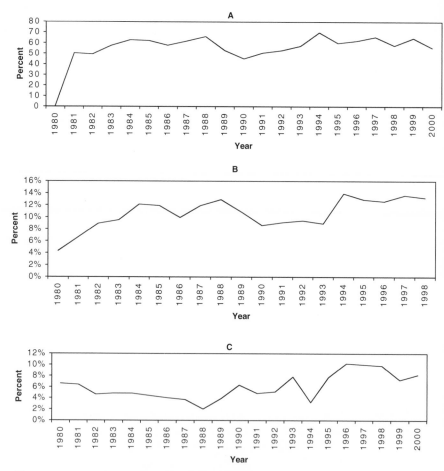

Figure 1.6. Change in External Sector Indicators (in %): Real Exchange Rate (A) Exports—GNP Ratio (B), and Foreign Trade—GNP Ratio (C).
Source: State Institute of Statistics, various issues.

respondingly, the share of non-OECD countries in Turkish trade decreased. Some hail this change as a desirable outcome, a boost to Turkey's longstanding bid to join the European Union. At the same time, it should be recognized that this concentration on OECD and the EU has increased Turkey's economic dependence and shaped not only the external sector but also the entire economy along the dictates of the industrial countries in these regions. Not surprisingly, the share of manufactured products in total exports jumped from 36 percent in 1980 to 79 percent in 1998 (OECD Economic Survey, var-

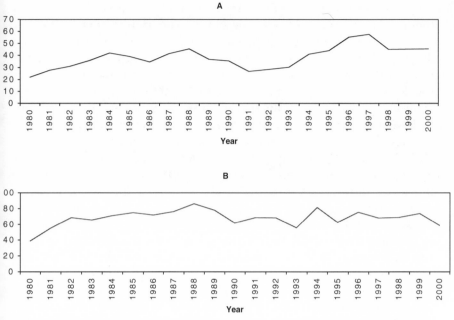

Figure 1.7. Openness Indicators, 1980–2000: Exports/Imports/GDP (A), and Exports/Imports (B).
Source: IMF, *International Financial Statistics,* and *OECD Economic Survey,* various issues.

ious issues). Similarly, the share of manufactured products in total imports increased from 53 percent in 1980 to 78 percent in 1998. Among the benefits of this shift, one could list factors such as the rise in value added, the improvement in terms-of-trade, industrialization, and the like. Two major problems, however, are the erosion of real wages in manufacturing and the subsequent increase in the income gap in the economy, and the contribution of industrialization to environmental degradation.

In the neoclassical open economy model, a successful real devaluation (or depreciation) inevitably leads, at least in the short-run, to a decrease in real wages, which in turn stimulates external competitiveness. Hence, structural adjustment programs emphasize wage flexibility, especially in a downward direction. Without this flexibility a real devaluation (or depreciation) would not increase profitability and production in the economy. The weakening of labor unions in the post-1980 era in Turkey has indeed helped to transform the labor market by bringing to it the necessary downward wage flexibility. In the 1980s, real wages declined by an annual average of 2 percent in the private sector and 1.1 percent in the public sector (OECD 1987/88, 20). The wage explosions of 1993 and 1994 were short-lived. In 1997, real wages in private sectors dropped to their 1990 level, and in the public sector they are only recently recovering from the lows they reached in 1996 (OECD 1999, 65). Specifically, in 1994–98, private and public sector gross wages dropped, on average, by 10.3 and 6.5 percent per year, respectively. In the same period, the average decrease in the minimum wage was about 2 percent per year (IMF 2000b, 102). The impact of this downward wage flexibility on unemployment has been limited, as seen in Figure 1.8. The unemployment figures more than double if underemployment is taken into account. The sum of unemployment and underemployment peaked in 1994 at 16.3 percent and decreased to 12.2 percent only in the late 1990s (IMF 2000b, 100). The labor market has been adversely affected by the contractionary policies that further raise unemployment by pushing demand down and contributing to an undesirable low output-large unemployment-low real wage spiral (Nas and Odekon 1998, 244).

During the 1980–98 period, the share of manufacturing in the GNP increased from 17 to 23.8 percent (SIS, various issues). This rise in manufacturing in GNP at the expense of agriculture, coupled with the overall real wage decline, is a major factor in explaining the rise in income inequality in Turkey. In 1987–94, the income share of the lowest quintile decreased from 5.2 to 4.9 percent whereas that of the top quintile increased from 49.9 to 54.9 percent (SIS 1987, 278; 1999, 662).

The primary effect of the increase in openness and in trade in manufactured goods was to raise the share of the manufacturing sector in the economy. In 1980, the share of manufacturing was 17 percent. It peaked in 1988–89 at 23 percent and stabilized around 21 percent in the late 1990s (SIS, various issues). Another interesting development was the change in the composition of manufacturing exports. Already by 1987, labor-intensive and scale-intensive industries constituted three quarters of total manufacturing exports (OECD Economic Survey 1989/90, 39). In the 1990s, the share of labor-intensive textile exports decreased to 38 percent from 46 percent in 1987, and the share of what OECD calls "differentiated goods" (for example, electrical appliances, metal products, and machinery) in total exports rose significantly on average (IMF 2000b, 108). Also, a move toward the export of high pollutant industry products (see chapter 4) has been a defining characteristic of Turkish openness. This change

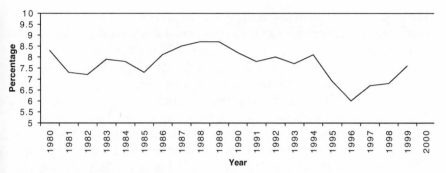

Figure 1.8. Unemployment Rate
Source: *OECD Economic Survey,* various issues and IMF 200a.

constitutes a good example of the indirect migration of high pollutant industries from its trading partners to Turkey. Rather than phys-
ically moving their high pollutant industries abroad, the Western
European economies encouraged high pollutant commodity production abroad with their high import demand and thereby exported their pollution abroad. In addition, the transfer of resources
embedded in the production of manufactured exports further blurs
the picture as to who really gains from openness and trade.

In addition, the sharp increase in openness and export/import ratios (see Figure 1.7) in the early 1980s has not been successfully sustained in later years. Even the most successful aspect of the liberalization program has met bottlenecks. Among the reasons for this
limited success one could point out the lack of a long-term export
promotion strategy in place. As a result, neither new export products
nor exploration of new export markets came about. Also, the liberalization of the capital account caused speculative short-term capital
inflows, appreciating the Turkish lira. Yenturk from TÜSIAD (Turkish Industrialists' and Businessmen's Association) writes, "New exporting sectors and investments were necessary to sustain the growth
in Turkey's exports. By then [1988], the effectiveness of devaluations
declined and the wages were reduced to rock bottom limits of social
acceptability. The period of promoting exports via short term policies was now over" (1997, 1). The loss in export competitiveness cost
the economy dearly. The external sector deficit increased significantly as discussed above. Furthermore, rising interest rates also
raised the cost of servicing the external debt. Once again, the authorities' "fix as you go along" approach to policy-making intensified

the external balance problems in the economy and to some extent was responsible for the 1994 and the post-1994 financial crises.

If Turkey intends to promote exports, it needs to go beyond the dictates of the IMF and the World Bank and carefully study the potential role of the state in this endeavor. The Asian tigers provide valuable lessons in that regard. As we have found out in the 1990s, to the Fund's and Bank's dismay, none of them have been "good" students of free trade theory. Active public policy in almost all spheres of economic life contributed to the success of the Asian tiger countries. Along with the economic incentives (that is, subsidies, tax breaks, etc.), institutional reforms to facilitate the penetration of export markets, export promotion zones, industrial parks, councils to increase the communication between the public and private sectors, and the setting and monitoring of export targets, to name a few, have all contributed to the successful implementation of export promotion strategies. These policies alone, however, would not have been enough. Political and economic stability is the prerequisite for the successful implementation of any development strategy. The Asian tigers were successful in their export orientation as long as macroeconomic stability prevailed. Otherwise, adverse developments in the economy affect investment and relative prices, and thus its financial stability, so the country loses its competitiveness in world markets and faces a series of crises.

The failure of the economic programs in Turkey manifests itself in the rising external debt. Turkey has had a long history of international indebtedness that it hoped to decrease to remain solvent by clinging to the IMF/World Bank economic reforms. Unfortunately, the financial gap, the sum of the current account deficit, debt-servicing charges, and the capital account shortfall has been steadily growing. Consequently, external indebtedness has been following a parallel trend. The financial gap in the 1980s hovered around $3 billion in the late 1980s and early 1990s. It has, however, steadily increased since 1993. In 1994, the financial gap increased to $10.5 billion, peaking in 2000 with a record 22.3 billion. Consequently, as can be seen in Figure 1.9, the share of the short-term debt in total debt, and the short-term debt-to-reserve-money ratio, increased significantly over time. In spite of the IMF/World Bank reforms, Turkey has been pushed more and more into short-term indebtedness, which in turn has raised the cost of debt servicing. The deterioration in the capital account in the beginning of 1993, and the far-below-expecta-

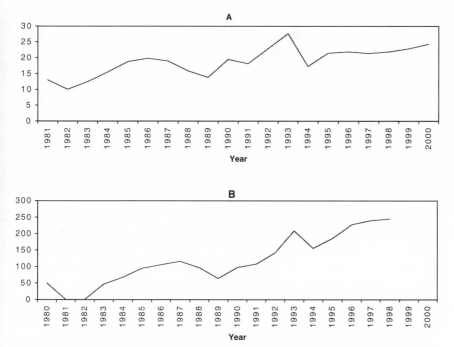

Figure 1.9. Debt Indicators, 1980–2000: Short-Term Debt/Total Debt (A), and Short-Term Debt-Reserve Money (B).
Source: IMF, International Financial Statistics, and *OECD Economic Survey*, various issues.

tions foreign capital inflows contributed to the ever-increasing financial gap and external indebtedness.

Performance criteria are among the most important measures for a country's compliance with the program commitments and thus are the basis for loan disbursements. The quantitative performance criteria are expressed in the form of ceilings/floors on variables such as primary balance, net domestic assets of the Central Bank, net international reserves, external debt, etc. In addition, performance criteria may also apply to proposed structural reforms, for example, privatization, and banking and tax reforms. Failure to meet the performance criteria may jeopardize the continuation of the program unless the IMF Executive Board approves a waiver. In certain cases, however, satisfying the performance criteria may not be enough to free the loan disbursements. If an IMF Program Review decides that the program is failing to meet its broader overall goals, even though it might meet individual targets, IMF may require remedial measures. Structural benchmarks and indicative targets are two additional assessment tools that IMF uses to monitor the success of a program. They are, however, less binding than the performance criteria.

The recent failures to meet the inflation targets are explained by the data on Turkey's compliance with the performance criteria as provided in the LoIs. The overall compliance with the quantitative performance criteria during March 2000–2001 is 80 percent. Noncompliance consistently was restricted to the excessive increase in the stock of net domestic assets of the Central Bank, the main reason for the increase in the monetary base and inflation. Recent compliance regarding the structural conditionalities also stands at a respectable 86 percent. Among the structural conditionalities not met are the liquidation of some Savings Deposit Insurance Fund banks, the halving of the number of revolving funds, the privatization of Turk Telecom, and the reduction of the stock of private sector tax arrears.

To conclude: Turkish authorities since 2000 have aggressively implemented the IMF program and have achieved important results. After all, the Fund, which is desperate to show the world an example of the success of its programs, renewed its commitment to Turkey by making it the most heavily indebted country to the Fund. In achieving this status, however, Turkish authorities have relentlessly closed their eyes and ears to the worsening of the economic conditions of the low- and middle-income classes.

There is no consensus on a theoretical framework to assess the impact of the IMF/World Bank policies on growth. In Appendix 1.A, the relationship between per capita income growth and three policy target variables (CPI inflation, budget surplus–GNP ratio, openness, and a dummy variable for post–1980 financial crises) are investigated using a simple model. As expected, inflation and financial crises have adverse effects on per capita growth, whereas openness has a small but positive impact.

The overview of post-1980 policies in this chapter has shown that Turkey had limited success with the liberalization programs in spite of the fact that Turkish authorities and the Turkish people worked hard to transform the economy into a market-oriented system with which they had limited experience. The IMF and the World Bank, along with the international financial community, repeatedly asked for more liberalization and for more austerity. They systematically failed to grasp that the imposed transition conflicted with statist cultural values and disrupted the rhythm of the economy in general. Consequently, ordinary people in the street became more and more victimized by the austerity programs and faced ever-increasing economic vulnerability. The pro-business, pro-multinational, and pro-speculator policies imposed by the IMF and the World Bank had a high price in terms of inequality and poverty. It is most urgent that these international organizations assume responsibility for designing policies targeting growth with equity. As we will discuss in Chapter 5, current policies focus on strengthening the role of the industrial core in the core-periphery relations in the new world economic system.

It would be irresponsible, on the other hand, not to agree with the fact that growth with equity cannot be realized unless fiscal deficits and inflation are controlled. The question is how to do it. Cutting real wages, social security, and privatization may not be the only choice. The brunt of all these is borne by the relatively vulnerable groups. In the case of Turkey, one of the main sources of fiscal deficit is military expenditures. A genuine attempt to curb fiscal deficits inevitably should focus on military spending, which in the 1990s amounted to 18–20 percent of the budget and about 3–4 percent of the GNP (SIS 1999). There is no need for Turkey to keep the largest armed force in NATO in Europe (about 800,000). The Turkish authorities must reevaluate Turkish military and defense needs, setting Turkey's own national priorities instead of following those of the NATO and the United States. Rationalization of the military and its expenditures should be preceded by a permanent peace agreement with the Kurds, now that the war has come to an end. In addition, the Cyprus conflict needs to be revisited, allowing the Turkish Cypriot people to decide their own sovereignty. The military leadership indeed may continue to overemphasize Kurdish as well as Greek threats because of self-interest. A strong political leadership with popular backing could convince the military otherwise.

Privatization, especially in the form of block sales of SEEs, is not the only available strategy to reduce the burden of the SEEs on the economy. Strengthening the economic role of the public sector by rendering it economically efficient and profitable may prove to be a more desirable strategy. The assumption that "private" is better than "public" is not a universally agreed-upon proposition. "Inefficient public" is inferior to "efficient private," the same way "efficient public" would be superior to "inefficient private." An alternative way of rendering the SEEs efficient could be the transfer of their ownership to the workers who are the primary stakeholders with a long-run self-interest into the success of the enterprise. Given the public sector's pivotal role in the Turkish economy since the foundation of the republic in 1923 and the relatively high human capital endowment of labor associated with this experience, it is conceivable that the Turkish labor could be able to participate more actively and successfully as the primary stakeholder in the production process in the public sector in the economy. An efficient public sector led by the self-interest guided labor could prove to be as successful as a privately run enterprise and could additionally help create revenues that could be spent on the public provision of basic needs and the much-needed improvement of the social, economic, and technological infrastructure. Additional revenue sources could also be secured from several tax levies. A tax levy on domestic and international financial transactions may also reduce financial speculation. Two recent financial crises have shown that the uncontrolled foreign financial flows have long-run repercussions. To eliminate these unwanted speculative runs, prudential rules for international investors need to be put into place. In addition, eliminating tax havens for domestic and international corporations and taxing the profits of multinationals are necessary measures to increase tax revenues and distribute the tax burden equitably. Sharing costs and benefits of growth and development equitably is the only way of achieving the socially and economically sustainable stability that investors look for. In sum, the promotion of the role of the public sector in the economy, and not its elimination, would secure the overall stability of the Turkish economy that would attract investors and foster growth and development.

2
Financial Liberalization

THE SAVINGS-INVESTMENT GAP IS ONE OF THE MAJOR BOTTLENECKS FOR growth in developing countries. Financial liberalization targets this excess demand for investment. From a neoclassical point of view, liberalizing financial markets stimulates domestic savings, foreign capital inflows, and hence physical capital formation, and consequently fosters economic growth. The structuralist paradigm, on the other hand, maintains that the deregulation of interest rates, a concomitant part of any financial liberalization package, raises the cost of borrowing and therefore, at least in the short run, may lower economic growth. Furthermore, according to Grabel, financial liberalization in Southern Cone countries has had adverse effects on economic growth because, "it creates new opportunities for non-productive profit-seeking and causes misallocation of credit toward speculative activities" (1995, 128).

This chapter reviews the important aspects of the Turkish experience with financial liberalization, and then assesses liberalization's effects on investment. In spite of the fact that certain financial reforms were necessary to strengthen the banking and financial sector to avoid insolvency, financial liberalization has also facilitated financial speculation diverting financial resources away from productive investment. First, the post–1980 reforms are summarized, then the role of foreign capital flows is examined, and the causes and consequences of Turkey's series of financial and banking crises in the 1998–2000 period are discussed. Finally, the impact of liberalization on investment is assessed.

POST–1980 FINANCIAL REFORMS

Financial liberalization results from the elimination of financial market regulations in order to increase microeconomic efficiency in the

53

economy (Anand and Wijnbergen 1988). Typically, in the preliberalization period, interest rates are regulated below their market rate, leading to negative real interest rates and financial repression, as shown in Figure 2.1. The regulated below-the-equilibrium interest rate, i_2, results in excess demand for investment and creates an opportunity for the economically and politically privileged to borrow at this regulated rate and then loan out at the high market demand rate, i_1, causing massive misallocation of financial resources. Under such conditions, large corporations in Turkey either formed their own banks to secure access to financial resources or borrowed from the regulated and inefficient commercial banking system at a high cost (Yeldan 1997). Deregulation of the interest rates eliminated this rent-creating situation, as shown in Figure 2.1, and raised interest rates to their equilibrium value at i_0, increasing the efficiency of the financial markets. Several studies show that such financial opening may provide significant benefits and affect the performance of the financial institutions (e.g., Barajas et al. 2000; Claasens et al. 1998).

The behavior of the three major real interest rates in Turkey is displayed in Figure 2.2. In the immediate aftermath of the launching of the liberalization program, the real interest rate on savings deposits and the Central Bank discount rate turned positive. However, by 1988

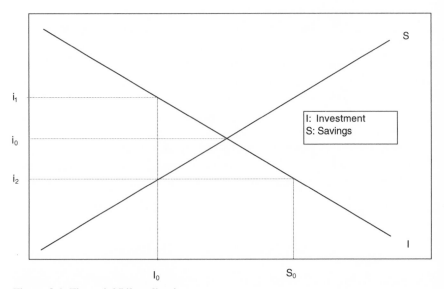

Figure 2.1. Financial Liberalization

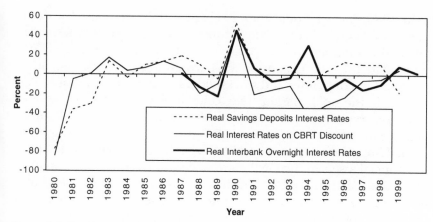

Figure 2.2. Real Interest Rates, 1980–2000
Source: IMF 2001d

they were again negative, as they were in 1994 and 1998. The real overnight interbank rate followed a similar pattern. The negative real interest rates were predominantly the result of continuing high inflation and of regulation of interest rates in the economy. Thus the liberalization of the financial markets in Turkey followed a stop-and-go pattern. For instance, the deregulation of deposit and lending rates in 1980 was short-lived, and was suspended with the collapse of financial markets in 1983. The well-documented brokerage-house crisis that led to the collapse resulted from the "uncontrolled" deregulation in effect in the 1980–83 period (Akyuz 1990; Atiyas 1990; Inselbag and Gultekin 1988; and OECD Ecomic Survey 1987/88, 63–84). The lack of an established legal and institutional framework enabled the brokerage firms to offer high interest rates that they could not afford. The Central Bank interfered and supported the banks, successfully preventing the crisis from spreading to the entire financial sector. In 1983, interest rate controls returned, along with other restrictions to stabilize the financial markets.

In the 1984–88 period, several new financial instruments (such as Income Sharing and Profit and Loss Sharing Certificates) were introduced along with significant institutional reforms to support the banking sector. The latter group includes: "provisions regarding the capital structure of the banks, the protection of deposits through an insurance plan and deposit insurance fund, the treatment of non-performing loans, and a standardized accounting system" (Inselbag and Gultekin 1988, 133).

In 1986, the Istanbul Stock Exchange (ISE) reopened with approximately eighty companies' stocks being traded. By the end of 2000, the number of companies traded on the stock exchange jumped to 287. This expansion was partially due to the tax incentives provided to companies and stockholders to encourage them to participate in the stock market (OECD Economic Survey 1987/88, 83). The policy worked and consequently the importance of financial markets in the economy increased. Figure 2.3 shows the rising ratio of total financial assets to the GNP. Especially from 1990 on, the share of financial assets in the GNP increased significantly, almost quadrupling their share in 1999. A different interpretation of the graph, however, suggests that a growth rate of financial assets higher than the growth of the real sector (GNP) represents the increasing speculative bubble in the economy. The relatively high share of financial assets indicates the persistent speculative bubble. Nevertheless, the Turkish bull market of 1989–90 has not repeated itself in the 1990s. The growth rates of the stock market traded value and of the number of stocks peaked in 1989–90 and stabilized after 1992 (Figures 2.4a and 2.4b). In fact, one could argue that the growth of capital markets in Turkey has been limited. Factors contributing to this slowness range from the fact that large family-owned companies have not rushed to go public to the lack of a large number of small financial investors who evaluate corporate financial statements and participate in the market. Indeed the ratio of stocks traded to the total volume of securities reached a peak in 1990 at 35 percent and has declined

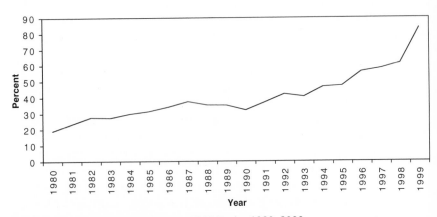

Figure 2.3. Total Financial Asset to GNP Ratio, 1980–2000
Source: Undersecreteriat of Treasury, *Treasury Statistics.*

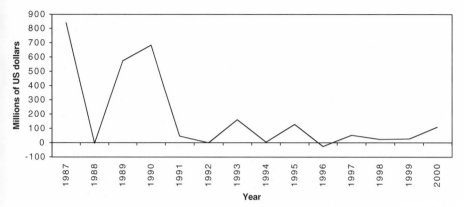

Figure 2.4a. Stock Market: Traded Value (millions US dollars), 1980–2000
Source: Undersecreteriat of Tresury, *Treasury Statistics.*

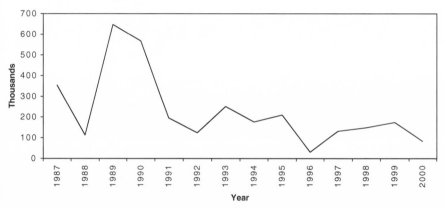

Figure 2.4b. Number of Stocks Traded (thousands), 1980–2000
Source: Undersecreteriat of Tresury, *Treasury Statistics.*

steadily since then (Undersecreteriat of the Treasury). In addition, as mentioned in the previous chapter, the public sector has traditionally been a heavy borrower in the economy, contributing to the limited growth of capital markets because of the high interest rates offered on government debt instruments.

The liberalization of financial markets, as expected, changed the financial portfolio of the economy significantly. Figures 2.5a and 2.5b on monetary aggregates show that the share of bank deposits in total financial assets declined steadily after 1980, with the share of sight

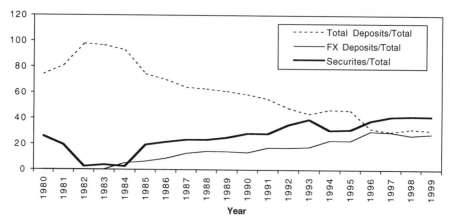

Figure 2.5a. Monetary Aggregates, 1980–2000
Source: Undersecreteriat of Tresury, *Treasury Statistics.*

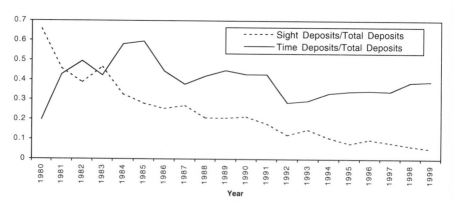

Figure 2.5b. Monetary Aggregates, 1980–2000
Source: Undersecreteriat of Tresury, *Treasury Statistics.*

deposits decreasing faster than that of time deposits, indicating that the public started substituting the new financial assets with high returns for traditional bank assets with relatively low returns. After 1992, however, the share of time deposits slightly increased, this time in response to increasing economic uncertainty. Rising riskiness and uncertainty also led to the dollarization of the economy. M2Y/GDP ratio increased sharply and the rise in M2Y lowered the M2/M2Y ratio substantially (Figures 2.5c and 2.5d). These ratios give only a rough estimate of the true magnitude of the dollarization since they

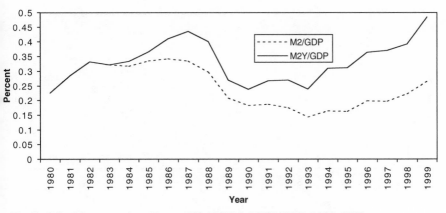

Figure 2.5c. Monetary Aggregates, M2/GDP & M2Y/GDP, 1980–2000
Source: Undersecreteriat of Tresury, *Treasury Statistics.*

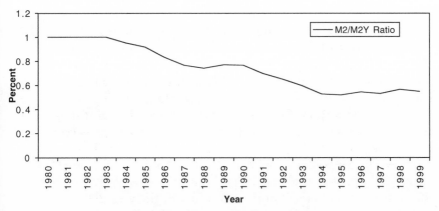

Figure 2.5d. Monetary Aggregates, M2/M2Y Ratio, 1980–2000
Source: Undersecreteriat of Tresury, *Treasury Statistics.*

do not account for the exact value of dollar transactions in the economy. Nevertheless, they point to the currency substitution that has taken place. Akcay et al. (1997) have estimated the extent of the dollarization and also shown a positive correlation between dollarization and the volatility of the exchange rate in Turkey, as proven in the post–1998 crises.

Liberalization of the financial markets, as expected, diminished the role of the Central Bank in credit creation. The share of Central Bank credit in the total credit stock (Figure 2.6) decreased steadily

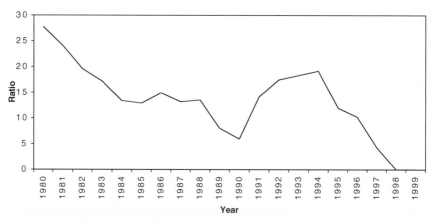

Figure 2.6. Total Central Bank Credits / Total Credit Ratio
Source: Undersecreteriat of Tresury, *Treasury Statistics.*

until 1986. As a result of the Central Bank's inability and/or unwillingness to control its credits, Central Bank credit increased again in
the post–1986 period until in 1995 its credit share surpassed its 1982
level. The growth rates of Central Bank and total credit in Figure 2.7
show explicitly the volatility of Central Bank credit. Only in the
1998–2000 period has Central Bank credit been brought under control. The total credit stock in the economy, however, has continued
to increase as banking sector credit completely replaced Central
Bank credit. Deposit money banks, public and private, which in the
early 1980s provided about 75 percent of the total credits, became
the only source of credit in the economy by the year 2000.

Additional measures in the financial liberalization package included new legislation geared to enhancing the competitiveness and
efficiency of bank and nonbank financial institutions. This legislation
also simplified the preferential credit system, and increased the supervisory role of the Capital Market Board created in 1981. It was only
after the 1998 crisis that the authorities finally realized the dangers
of financial liberalization without first putting strong supervisory and
regulatory institutions first in place.

In 1987, the Central Bank began to engage in open market operations in a very restrictive manner, and took the first steps to create a
foreign exchange market. In the early 1980s foreign banks were allowed to open branches, and accordingly the handling of foreign exchange transactions was transferred from the Central Bank to com-

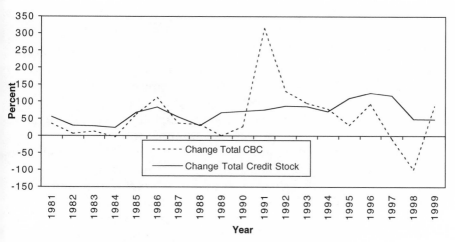

Figure 2.7. Change in Central Bank Credit and Total Credit Stock
Source: Undersecreteriat of Tresury, *Treasury Statistics.*

mercial banks. In addition, again in a stop-and-go fashion, Turkish citizens were allowed to open foreign exchange accounts and to engage in foreign exchange transactions. The liberalization of the capital account facilitated foreign investors and funds to enter Turkish markets and also allowed Turkish investors to buy foreign assets worth up to $5,000 (Esen 2000). The 1991 Gulf War and elections slowed down the financial reform attempts considerably. The only noteworthy undertaking in this period was the authorization of the Capital Market Board to supervise and regulate financial markets. These reforms, however, could not prevent the 1994 and 1999–2000 financial crises. Loss of confidence in the financial markets and economic policies alike triggered a massive currency substitution, which ultimately led to the collapse of the Turkish lira. In April 1994, new measures were introduced to contain the financial and economic effects of the crisis and to restore confidence in the system. Public expenditure cuts, tax reforms, the resumption of Treasury borrowing in the financial markets, the buildup of foreign reserves, and the 1995 economic upturn helped thwart the crisis. In 1999 and 2000, speculation and arbitrage transactions diverted financial resources away from productive investment and toward government paper in particular. The distortion this diversion created in the markets led eventually to financial and banking crises by the end of 2000.

CAPITAL ACCOUNT LIBERALIZATION

The capital account in Turkey was liberalized in 1989. Several arguments support capital account liberalization. Within the neoclassical paradigm, such liberalization would cause efficient allocation of international financial resources, benefiting all countries importing or exporting capital. The inflow of foreign capital would also complement domestic saving by providing additional foreign currency denominated financial instruments, and hence would contribute to higher saving, investment, and income. Capital inflows also would encourage growth by bringing along foreign technology and management skills. Finally, foreign capital would compete with domestic capital, and the increased competition would lower the cost of borrowing. Nevertheless, volumes have been written on the sequencing and timing of capital account liberalization. Whether capital account liberalization should precede current account liberalization or whether domestic financial and exchange rate reforms (including convertibility) should be completed before opening up the capital account is still discussed extensively. For developing countries, foreign capital inflows may not be as beneficial as one might think. The inflow of foreign capital may take the form of the speculative portfolio investment, which could destabilize financial markets, and even more desirable direct investment may affect domestic savings adversely by raising consumption (Bosworth and Collins 1999). Furman and Stiglitz (1998) argue that to assess the future course of foreign capital inflow, authorities need to look at two main criteria, whether the inflows are permanent or temporary, and whether domestic or external factors are causing the inflows of capital. For instance, capital account liberalization could cause large temporary inflows as adjustment in the stock of capital takes place. Hence, speculative and nonproductive capital inflows may not affect capital formation.

Furthermore, in a pegged exchange rate regime, like Turkey's, high-powered money is the sum of Central Bank credit and international reserves. Hence, large inflows of capital would increase the international reserves, and unless sterilized, would also raise the money supply. The latter would intensify inflationary pressures (Furman and Stiglitz 1998, 23). Sterilization in this case, on the other hand, requires contractionary macroeconomic policies and therefore would increase the interest rates. Developing countries with large public and current account deficits must choose the lesser of the two evils, higher inflation or higher interest rates.

On the other hand, in a floating exchange rate regime, capital inflows would cause the exchange rate to appreciate and would affect
current account adversely. In short, capital inflows have to be managed with well-balanced, and fine-tuned macroeconomic policies for
the recipient developing country to reap their benefits.

In the Turkish case, current account liberalization has preceded
capital account liberalization. Not until 1984 could residents buy foreign currency directly from the banks. The pre–1980 balance of payments difficulties and foreign exchange shortages had led the authorities to put strict capital controls in effect. Private capital
outflows, for all practical purposes, were outlawed. The entry of foreign capital was closely supervised and the existing regulations and
high taxes served as strong enough disincentives that foreign and
capital inflow remained minimal. In 1989, encouraged by the current
account surplus, the policymakers liberalized the capital account,
eliminating almost all barriers to the free movement of capital. The
decision has resulted in an increase in actual (realized) foreign investment, as seen in Figure 2.8, which shows the ratio of actual (realized) foreign investment to total foreign investment permits. The
sharp increase in 1989–92 has not been sustained, and the ratio
decreased from 1993 to 1996. The high variation continued and the
ratio fluctuated widely. According to the Turkish Treasury, in the last
two decades the countries that had a relatively high foreign investment share in Turkey were France (17 percent), Germany (14 per-

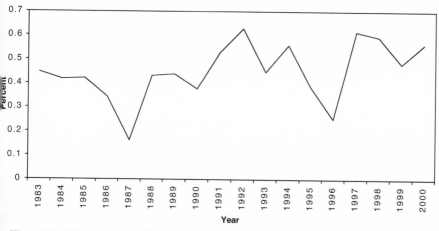

Figure 2.8. Ratio of Actual Foreign Investment to Total (in %)
Source: Undersecreteriat of Tresury, *Treasury Statistics.*

cent), Holland (13 percent), and the United States (12 percent) (Undersecreteriat of the Treasury). According to the data on its sectoral distribution, 54 percent of total foreign investment was in manufacturing and 43 percent in the service sector. Figures 2.9 and 2.10 give the breakdown of capital inflows according to their types. Foreign direct investment has been consistently lower than portfolio investment and other investment liabilities, for example, loans and credits. Banks have been the primary source of loans and credits, followed by foreign governments and monetary authorities. The figures are in accord with Celasun et al.'s findings (1997) that Turkey has not been a large capital importer, net foreign direct investment has been small, and loans and credits made to the nonfinancial sector have mostly been larger than the portfolio investment. Nevertheless, the marginal increase in portfolio investment and other investment liabilities came accompanied by increased vulnerability. Table 2.1 reveals the volatility of foreign investment and shows the mean and the standard deviation of the inflows for two subperiods, 1980–89 and 1990–2000. The volatility of portfolio investment relative to direct investment is significantly higher, and the volatility of loans and credits is even higher. Considering that this propensity for high volatility reflected the speculative appetite of foreign investors, one could argue it was a blessing that foreign capital inflow to Turkey was limited. As we will see below, even this limited inflow proved too effective in fueling the November 2000 crisis.

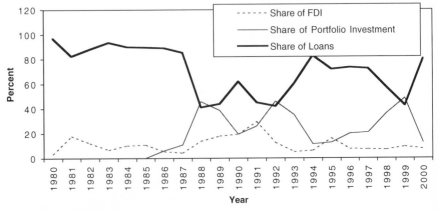

Figure 2.9. Capital Inflows (in %)
Source: IMF 2001d.

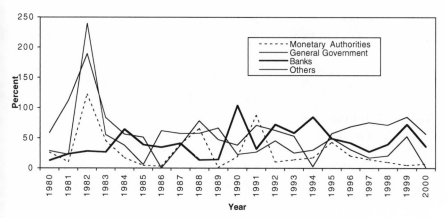

Figure 2.10. Breakdown of Other Investment Liabilities
Source: IMF 2001d.

It should not be denied, however, that direct and portfolio investment had a small but statistically significant effect on total investment in Turkey (Odekon 2003). Even though the effect of direct investment on total investment is significantly higher than that of portfolio investment, it is much less than reported in similar studies (see Bosworth and Collins 1999). In addition, the model fails to show any significant effects of the same inflows on saving. The lack of impact on saving could well mean that foreign capital inflow has led to the aforementioned domestic saving-consumption trade-off and therefore had no significant impact on domestic saving.

Turkish authorities have been very sympathetic to foreign capital in the post–1980s. In a short period of time the 1989 reforms have successfully targeted the anti–foreign capital bias in the economy and

Table 2.1. Volatility of Foreign Investment

1980–89	FDI	Portfolio	Other Investment
Mean	168.3	770.5	1121.2
Standard Deviation	196.5	640.5	725.4
1990–2000			
Mean	790.8	2368.5	5818.3
Standard Deviation	120.3	1626.9	3072.6

Source: IMF 2001d.

eliminated the barriers to the free entry and exit of foreign capital. The stable economic environment the IMF/World Bank liberalization and stabilization programs create, along with wage moderation, flexible organization of work, and business tax cuts Turkish LoIs commit themselves to, all aim to raise the attractiveness of the economy to private investment. After all, it is important to create an economy, especially financial market, which would make foreign investors feel at home. On behalf of the international financial markets, the IMF and the World Bank make sure that the principle of free entry and exit is established and that institutional restructuring is undertaken to free the markets from potential government supervision and to open new profitable investment opportunities for foreign investors. In a way, the approval of IMF credit signals the international financial community (for instance, in Turkey's case, the Paris Consortium) that the IMF and the World Bank endorse the country's creditworthiness in the markets. The criteria for creditworthiness are discussed in minute detail by invited business and political leaders at international meetings organized by the IMF, the World Bank, or the World Trade Organization in New York, Seattle, Quebec City, Davos, Dubai, Barcelona, Washington, DC, and elsewhere. Furthermore, to ensure continued stability, the IMF also commits itself to periodic expert visits to assess the country's compliance with the liberalization program. These visits serve as an early warning system, since a noncompliance report may signal increasing riskiness and lead to instantaneous reversal of the flows to minimize any potential losses.

In Turkey, the appointment of the new Minister of State for Economic Affairs in mid-2001 marked a change in the tone in the Turkish letters of intent sent to the IMF. Whereas the June 26 and July 31, 2001 LoIs talked about improving the business climate in general terms, referring explicitly only to the World Bank's and International Finance Corporation's (IFC) Foreign Investment Advisory Service (FIAS) review of the Turkish administrative barriers to investment, the September 20, 2001 LoI outlined the preparations for an "investor conference that will bring together major international business leaders. This will enhance our communication of our economic program to domestic and international financial markets, and encourage FDI [foreign direct investment]" (LoI, 2001, 20, September 8). Incidentally, the Turkish Treasury web page recently posted a document titled "The Enhancement of Investment Environment." The report refers to the Global Competitiveness Report prepared by the World Economic Forum (Davos meetings), which proves how the existing administrative barriers have lowered Turkey's competitiveness in the foreign investment markets.

On September 10–11, 2001, the FIAS and IFC participated in the presentation of an investment report at the Turkish Treasury and co-drafted an action plan incorporating the following (LoI, January 28, 2002, 13), submitting to the parliament a law regulating foreign direct investment and another regulating the employment of foreign personnel by foreign companies, and establishing an employee code of ethical conduct for customs proceedings. These reforms and the initiatives to enhance private investment culminated in a recent letter of intent: "Finally, to promote Turkey as an investment destination and learn from international perspectives, we have scheduled the inaugural meeting of the Investor Council for July 2002. Once established, we foresee that the Council, consisting of top-level officials of major international corporations, will meet annually" (LoI, April 3, 2002, 5).

It is to be kept in mind that the advantages and disadvantages of foreign capital and investment depend on the conditions imposed by the receiving economy and by the incoming foreign capital. In Turkey, domestic business and labor groups have barely discussed the pros and cons of foreign capital and investment in a substantive way, and the unconditional welcoming attitude of certain circles as if foreign capital and investment are the only remedy for the ills of the economy, to say the least, are thought provoking. It should be remembered that foreign capital moves across borders to minimize financial risk and to secure a higher return. The benefits of foreign capital and investment, on the other hand, depend on their impact on domestic investment, which has been weak in Turkey.

A possible additional adverse effect of financial liberalization could be its impact on the banking sector, to which we turn in the next section.

THE FINANCIAL CRISES

The main characteristic of Turkish financial portfolios in the 1980s was their disproportionately high share of government debt instruments, that is, public sector securities (bills and bonds). The high interest rates on these instruments, resulting from high and persistent fiscal deficits, created an atmosphere where banks made lucrative and stable profits merely by channeling private financial resources to government paper. Shirreff, in a 1997 article in *Euromoney*, claimed that Turkish banks were the most profitable in the world because the Turkish government rewarded them royally for making the Turkish citizens pay for the public debt. In addition, chronic inflation raised the demand for banks' transaction services and contributed to their reported accounting profits. Indeed, comparative financial indicators rank Turkish banks among the most successful in Europe. According to the IMF (2000b), Turkish banks' 1994–96 profits before taxes, scaled by average assets, were 5.3 percent, followed by Poland (3.7 percent) and Germany (1 percent). In the same time period, a main contributor to the profits, the net interest margin scaled by the assets in Turkey stood at 8.6 percent, followed again by Poland (3.5 percent). However, Turkish banks operate at an enormous cost. Their operating expenses in 1994–96 were highest in Europe, 3.9 percent, mainly because of high staff costs. Staff costs were 31.9 percent, considerably higher than Poland, with 27.4 percent. Consequently, Turkish banks' staff costs relative to average assets were twice Poland's, 2.8 and 1.9 respectively. Certainly, the tendency of the banks to open up branches for promotional purposes contributed to the high personnel costs. Turkish banks have 99.6 branches per million population, again ranking highest in Europe, followed by Germany with eighty-nine branches. These figures draw the profile of the Turkish banking. Banks are highly profitable thanks to high interest earnings from public debt instruments but at the same time quite fragile because of high operating costs. In the 1980s and 1990s, the banks also exposed themselves to high exchange risks. They borrowed heavily in international markets to use foreign currency to buy the government debt instruments offering high domestic yields. However, they thereby exposed themselves to exchange risk (in the case of devaluation/depreciation) and interest rate risk (in the case of deflation/falling interest rates). Over time, as disinflationary policies lowered interest rates and devaluations raised the domestic currency value of foreign loans, the exchange and interest risks started exerting themselves.

The first financial crisis in the 1990s hit the economy in 1994. The continuing fiscal deficit caused financial markets to lose confidence in the Turkish lira and there was a massive currency substitution as shown by the sharply rising M2Y/GDP ratio in the central graph in Figure 2.5c. The Turkish lira depreciated by more than 60 percent within a month (more than 130 percent annually). This sudden loss of value forced banks with short-term open positions in foreign currency to lose large amounts of their capital (OECD Economic Survey 1995, 23). The Central Bank's intervention helped restore investors' confidence, and the banking sector survived the scare of 1994. New reserve and liquidity requirements, new financial instruments to compete with foreign exchange accounts, and guarantees of individual bank deposits were among the new policy measures taken in 1994.

The 1994 crisis was not the only one Turkey would face in the post–1980 liberalization era. To some extent, financial liberalization created the crises since it tends to hurt the banking sector in developing countries. As the Bank of International Settlements (1997, 13) argued, increased competition in the financial sector may push banks to undertake riskier investments without the necessary expertise to deal with these risks and may lead banks to extend credit for inferior projects. Especially smaller, inexperienced banks were victimized by financial and economic liberalization. Decrease in the primary fiscal deficits, in inflation, in interest rates and lower interest spreads pushed the banks into activities they were not familiar with, consumer lending. Their financial positions worsened as more and more foreign banks and nonbank institutions entered the market. Currently, around twenty foreign banks operate in Turkey, as opposed to four in the 1980s. This fivefold increase inevitably raised competition, with all the attendant pros and cons. By the end of the year 2000, twenty-seven domestic commercial banks accounted for 50 percent of banking assets, with the four largest banks, owned by holding companies, controlling 28 percent.

The scars of the 1994 crisis in Turkey healed quickly. The subsequent Tequila Crisis of 1994–95 and the 1997 East Asian crises did not affect the Turkish economy. With little Turkish investment in bonds denominated by Mexican peso or Thai bath, these crises had no contagion effects in Turkey. The 1998 Russian crisis, however, led to an immediate worsening of export performance, causing significant outflow of capital (by about $7 billion) and reducing the foreign reserves by $2 to $3 billion (OECD Economic Survey 1999, 34). The subsequent liquidity squeeze contracted the economy as interest rates rose. Luckily the banking sector's overall open exchange position in 1998 was less open than at the 1994 crisis, limiting the depth and duration of the 1998 crisis. Nevertheless, smaller banks suffered because of some exposure to foreign exchange and interest rate risks.

The rising interest rates also took their toll on the state-run banks. As mentioned previously, these banks engaged in semi-fiscal transactions on behalf of the treasury and as a result accumulated massive unpaid duty losses. They already faced declining profits through losing their market share to increased competition. Rising interest rates in 1998 significantly enlarged the wedge between their cost of borrowing and the low interest loans they provided to the public enterprises. These developments further pushed up market interest rates, since these banks had to borrow heavily to finance their loan activities.

The vulnerability and fragility of the banking system did not prevent some banks from assuming high exchange and interest rate risks and thus engaging in speculative and uncovered arbitrage activities. Under these circumstances the 1999 earthquake and the 2000 political crisis helped plunge the Turkish economy into the severe banking crisis of 2000, characterized by significant bank losses and weakened solvency. The economic slowdown and the resulting corporate financial difficulties further deepened the banking crisis.

A series of reforms to restructure the banking sector had already been introduced at the 1994 crisis. The reforms aimed to strengthen the financial system by increasing supervision in the financial markets in line with international norms, and liquidating or merging insolvent institutions. They also attempted to ensure that financial institutions' solvency by enforcing capital adequacy requirements. These measures implicitly assume that big private financial institutions are more efficient and therefore more desirable. The letters of intent of 1998–2000 continued focusing on these four areas and incorporated additional policy measures aiming to assure the international financial community that Turkish financial markets would be restructured to welcome them. In addition to standardizing the regulations of bank and nonbank financial institutions to make them competitive, supervisory reforms were put in place to facilitate the financial institutions' adjustment to the new financial regime, characterized by the coexistence of domestic and foreign financial institutions and low public deficit, low inflation and low interest rates. In 1999, the new Banking Regulation and Supervision Agency (BRSA) incorporated the relevant departments of the Central Bank and the Treasury. This new agency was responsible for strengthening banking discipline and guaranteeing confidence in banks (LoI, December 18, 2000, 10). The agency also had the legal leverage to intervene with banks whenever necessary to minimize the financial costs of bank failures. "Within a short period of time BRSA took control of ten banks to subsequently sell them" (LoI, December 9, 1999, 14). A review of the financial conditions of the private deposit banks and the letters of intent they had submitted, led to recapitalization by several banks and to the liquidation of a few (LoI 2001, June 26). Banks that could not raise sufficient capital were banned from merging with larger banks and liquidated (or resolved, in the contemporary parlance).

As mentioned in Chapter 1, the two state-owned banks, Ziraat and Halk, have for a while been prime targets for privatization on the basis of the argument that they make politically driven loans to specific sectors in the economy and hence distort the financial markets (OECD Economic Survey 1999, 126). OECD advice since 1994 has been to take lessons from the other OECD countries and rationalize and restructure the Turkish banking sector along similar lines. In particular, OECD claimed, the privatization of these state banks would significantly increase financial sector efficiency. The Turkish state banks had a large share in the sector. In 1998, they held approximately 40 percent of the banking sector's total assets and 41 percent of total deposits (IMF 2000b, 40). Instead of a gradual approach, the authorities once again chose to rush the privatization of the state banks. Both Ziraat and Halk were subject to abrupt radical changes. Their capital base was rebuilt in a relatively short period of time and their role as quasifiscal lenders was limited. Their staff has been reduced by 20 percent as a result of the closing of branches (LoI, January 28, 2002, 9). According to the April 3, 2002 LoI, "458 Ziraat and 369 Halk branches are or will be closed." These radical reforms had one aim: to privatize after the banks were solvent and commercialized. But again, the question becomes if they are already solvent, commercialized, and profitable, why privatize them? Why could they not remain as profitable state banks, serving the relatively small agricultural and/or nonagricultural producers in the economy? The answer to this question is obvious: the widespread faith that private is better than public. In the case of the Ziraat Bank, privatization would cut off credit to the state economic enterprises in agriculture and hence agricultural privatization would be facilitated as well.

Finally, all these reforms have been supplemented by measures designed to make corporations financially solvent also. The January 28, 2002, LoI emphasized two important aspects of corporate debt restructuring, some outstanding debt (especially that of Halk Bank) would be renegotiated at market terms, and the companies would adopt international accounting standards in their financial disclosures. Additional measures concerning the institutional, legal, and judicial framework ranged from the formation of an arbitration panel to solve disputes, to the formation of expert banks and the preparation of a new bankruptcy law.

As a result of these broad categories of reforms it was and still is hoped that the financial sector would be crisis-free. However, the Turkish financial system has been more vulnerable and fragile after the financial liberalization than ever before. As Bosworth and Collins (1999, 144–45) argued, financial liberalization has added risks to financial markets in developing countries. The Turkish financial markets were not an exception.

FINANCIAL LIBERALIZATION AND INVESTMENT

The success of economic liberalization programs, especially of financial liberalization, depends heavily on how investment responds to market reforms. The removal of price and non-price barriers can lead to an efficient allocation of resources, while the establishment of financial markets and interest rate liberalization should stimulate savings. Both of these developments, especially in the long run, contribute to increased investment in the economy. According to the findings by Henry (2000), financial market liberalization has led to private investment booms and created a strong positive relationship between stock market evaluation and private investment, even though, as the author admits, world economic performance may have helped the investment boom. In the case of Turkey, Guncavdi et al. (1998) provided evidence that financial liberalization has stimulated changes in investment functions, but could not definitely argue for a significant positive relationship between the two.

Fixed capital formation has generally not been strong in Turkey. Table 2.2 distinguishes among total, public, and private fixed business investment to GDP ratios. Evidently, privatization has taken its toll on public investment, even though in the late 1990s the share of public investment in the GDP increased. The private investment–GDP ratio, on the other hand, decreased in 2000 to its 1980 level. Historically, agriculture, transportation, and education have been areas that attracted public investment. Private investors preferred energy, housing, manufacturing, and since mid–1990, as a result of privatization in the sector, transportation as well.

The fact that in two decades the total investment–GDP ratio has not significantly changed is telling in terms of the impact of financial liberalization on investment. Financial liberalization increased the number and variety of financial instruments in the Turkish economy. However, the extent to which this increase has contributed to private

Table 2.2. Public and Private Fixed Business Investment–GDP Ratios

	1975–79	1980	1996	2000
Total Investment/ GDP	24.3	21.8	25.0	22.5
Public Investment/ GDP	8.6	8.7	5.1	6.9
Private Investment/ GDP	13.1	15.7	19.9	15.6

Source: *OECD Economic Survey,* various issues.

capital formation in the manufacturing sector is ambiguous. The literature claims that in the postliberalization era manufacturing firms, especially large ones, rely more and more on external funding sources for investment expenditures (*Economist* 1995, 80; Athey and Laumas 1994). Fazzari et al. (1988, 148) argued that internal and external capital are not perfectly interchangeable, and that firms compare the costs of internal and external funds. Asymmetric information, transportation costs, taxes, and financial distress can cause external funds to have high costs and make firms choose internal funds for investment.

Turkish data on various financial market liberalization indicators is scarce. Nevertheless, a simple accelerator model of investment is used here to measure the effects of internal and external financing sources on investment. The accelerator model of manufacturing investment postulates that investment responds to current and lagged sales, ΔS and $\Delta S(-1)$, respectively, and changes in profits, $\Delta \pi$, as the major internal sources for finance. A modified version of this model, tested here, incorporates the real interest rate, i, and a stock-market variable, *FIN*, as the external sources for finance. The results are presented in the Appendix 2.A. According to these findings, between 1986 and 1998 large manufacturing firms relied heavily on internal financing rather than borrowing from external sources as depicted by the significant coefficients on sales and profit variables. Real interest rate and the stock market variable have no significant effects on firms' investment decisions.

These findings call for a reevaluation of the results of financial liberalization. It seems that, at least in the 1986–98 period, the creation of a stock market in Turkey did not have the expected "resource" effect, and failed to close the increasing investment-saving gap in the economy. The substantial increase in the number of shares quoted in the stock market, as well as the sharp rise in the value of trading in the market, failed to affect investment as much as expected. A possible explanation could indeed be that the formation of the stock market siphoned funds away from productive physical capital formation and into speculation. Thus the "speculative" effect of financial liberalization has outweighed its "resource" effect. Measures need to be taken to redirect investment funds from speculative financial activity back to productive investment.

The IMF regularly has blamed the developing countries for financial crises. It has argued that either corruption or inappropriate policies or worsening macroeconomic fundamentals resulting from external shocks explain the postliberalization financial crises. This diagnosis has always led the IMF to push the developing countries with renewed energy toward public sector restructuring. Nobody can indeed deny the importance of public as well as private sector accountability and transparency. Neither can anyone deny that inherent financial market instability requires a strong regulatory and supervisory institutional framework (Minsky 1986). One inevitably wonders why the IMF/World Bank experts pushed for financial liberalization in Turkey or elsewhere in the developing world without first guaranteeing that the needed supervisory and regulatory mechanisms were in place. Clearly some kind of mechanism is needed to hold the IMF/World Bank accountable for misguided policy recommendations. Until recently, for example, the IMF recommended fixed exchange rates to control inflation, but had miscalculated the impact fixed rates would have on financial and other markets in the developing economies. To some extent, the recent Argentine crisis is the Fund's doing.

It would not be fair to Argentina to compare its crisis to the Turkish crisis. Argentina lacked the political and strategic leverage that Turkey had in the aftermath of September 11, 2001. The United States and the IMF approached the Turkish crisis very differently. Desperately seeking the Turkish alliance in its push for the war against Iraq, the United States has given the IMF the green light to provide the Turkish banking system with loans to avoid insolvency. According to the United States, Turkey not only is a loyal ally as NATO's point-base in the Middle East, but also is home to the military bases needed for the war against Iraq. Similarly, in late 2002, the United States interfered on behalf of Turkey in the Copenhagen European Council meeting on the enlargement of the European Union, lobbying heavily for Turkey's full membership. Argentina lacked a similar military and strategic importance for the United States.

The successful liberalization of financial markets and of the capital account demands a sound banking system, strictly regulated and supervised, as it is the case in industrial countries. As foreign banks move in, thanks to financial liberalization, domestic banks, as we have seen, may weaken, giving the economy a vulnerability and fragility that was not there before. In addition, as Singer points out, "domestic banks are more sensitive to subtle forms of influence by the central bank, for example, to expand credit when the economy needs stimulus and contract it when there are signs of overheating. Foreign banks are far less likely to be responsive to such signals" (1999, 70). In the economies accustomed to this kind of informal policy implementation, the changes that occur with financial liberalization can create heavy adjustment costs. Such adjustment costs aggravate the problems associated with financial liberalization, necessitating measures to minimize their impact. A more gradual liberalization could be a step in the right direction.

Transparency in government activity—that is, in drafting laws, setting regulations and supervisory rules, and in policy formulation and implementation—is of utmost importance in all IMF-developing country interactions. Transparency is almost a prerequisite for foreign capital to come to developing countries. However, the IMF fails to insist that similar rules of transparency apply to the foreign investors as well. For example, the conditions attached to foreign investment should be known by each agent in the host economy, by the entire business community as well as by the labor groups. In the case of Turkey, the business and labor groups should be fully informed about the Phillip Morris tobacco company, to cite a key instance, so that they can evaluate the implications of the provision that if the company produces over 1 million cigarettes in Turkey, it could import its other products produced elsewhere. Phillip Morris is part of a conglomerate that owns the Kraft food giant, among others. The potential penetration of Kraft foods into Turkey may jeopardize domestic firms in the industry. If these firms had part in a democratic decision-making process, they could be informed about future competition and take measures to strengthen their operations.

We mentioned before that for capital inflow to benefit the host country, permanency of the flow is important. The rapid entry and exit of speculative portfolio flows may impact the developing economies adversely. In order to limit these kinds of speculative transactions and their undesired effects on the economy, and to en-

sure permanency of the foreign capital inflow, a disincentive system
to discourage capital from leaving can be instituted. An exit tax (or
Tobin tax) immediately comes to mind as one element of an effective disincentive system to curb speculative attacks.

Efficient financial markets and a solvent banking system are two
important prerequisites for Turkey's membership in the European
Union. Efficiency and solvency, however, do not necessarily corre-
spond to full liberalization of the financial markets and privatization
of financial institutions. As we have repeatedly pointed out, the efficiency and solvency criteria can be met with capital controls and state-
owned financial institutions. For example, Credit Lyonnaise is one of
the largest banks in France and is owned by the state. In addition, several developing countries, for example East Asian tigers, have been
quite successful with capital controls in place. On the other hand, several privately owned financial institutions go bankrupt every year.

The Turkish financial sector needs reforms. However, these reforms do not necessarily mean complete privatization of state-owned
banks and full liberalization of the financial markets. In Turkey, as
elsewhere, deviations from freely functioning markets in the financial sector may curb the adverse economic and social costs of abrupt
liberalization and privatization.

After about twenty years of experimenting with financial market
and capital account liberalization, the IMF and the World Bank do
not seem to have completely mastered the interconnections among
the various policy recommendations they make. It is a pity that the
IMF and the World Bank continuously subject developing countries
to trial-and-error–based policy recommendations, while successfully
escaping accountability and responsibility.

3

De-agriculturalization

Economic liberalization had devastating socioeconomic effects on the agricultural sector in Turkey. The proindustrialization bias in the liberalization program significantly decreased the share of agriculture in the economy and reshaped the agricultural sector in line with the international division of labor in agriculture as dictated by the industrial countries, whereby industrial countries specialize in capital- and technology-intensive agricultural production and developing countries in labor-intensive vegetable and fruit production. Turkey, a historically net agricultural goods exporter and once the breadbasket of Europe, became a cereal importer within a short period of time. Chapter 3 begins with an overview of the important aspects of the agricultural sector in Turkey, then analyzes agricultural public policy and its effects on the sector. The hypothesis concerning the international division of labor in agriculture is introduced and discussed and the chapter closes with policy recommendations.

Overview

Structural change in agriculture is an expected outcome of growth and development. Economic development, theoretically, is expected to be accompanied by the introduction of new technology and methods that would raise productivity to guarantee sufficient agricultural production to support urbanization and industrialization. The post–1980 evolution of de-agriculturalization in Turkey runs counter to this goal.

Turkey has traditionally had an agricultural economy. In 1965, the country's rural population was 65.58 percent. By 1980, the figure had decreased to 56 percent. The latest available statistics (SIS 2000) show that in the last two decades, the share of rural population has dropped to 41 percent, still relatively high. Accordingly, the percentage of the population economically active in agriculture decreased from 72 percent in 1965 to 60 percent in 1980 and to 53.66 percent by the mid-1990s, with the share of women in the rural labor force hovering around 40 to 45 percent of the total rural labor force. According to the 1990 census, as a result of rapid urbanization, about 60 percent of the population lived in the cities. The average annual rate of urbanization in 1980–89 was a staggering 20 percent (SIS, 1993, 54–55). However, urbanization is concentrated in western Turkey while eastern and Southeastern regions of the country have experienced massive net emigration due to the Kurdish dispute. In the 1990–97 period, cities like Bitlis, Diyarbakir, and Hakkari had a population decrease of 15 to 35 percent, mostly men (SIS 1999, 63–65).

Another significant aspect of this rapid urbanization is that relatively young people, ages fifteen to twenty-nine, are leaving the rural areas, aggravating the problems facing the agricultural sector. In the long run, the aging rural population could magnify the agricultural human resource problems and further limit the sector's productivity and growth potential. Consequently, the rising incidence of child labor in rural areas is not surprising. According to the OECD Economic Survey (1996, 89), 16 percent of children between six and nine years old are engaged in work in rural areas to make up for the decline in the adult labor force in agriculture.

The dramatic drop in the share of agriculture in the GNP is the most telling evidence of the extent of the de-agriculturalization Turkey has experienced. Figure 3.1 displays the share of agriculture in GNP in constant prices. It rapidly declined in the 1980s. The decrease slowed in the 1990s, but by 1997 the share of agriculture had already been reduced to 12.7 percent. This decrease would not have been alarming if productivity in agriculture had increased. But one of the several factors that contributed to de-agriculturalization is the lagging growth of agricultural productivity. Slow introduction and adoption of new technology causes low agricultural productivity growth. OECD (OECD Economic Survey 1993, 46) estimates that labor productivity in agriculture in the early 1990s was 20 to 25 percent lower than that in manufacturing. Available data on agricultural equipment in use in 1990–99 reveal that even though the use of modern agricultural equipment rose (Table 3.1), farming still relied on a disproportionately large amount of nonmodern equipment. The data show that traditional agricultural methods are slowly being replaced by modern methods. The use of tractors in the last two decades has doubled. Because of the rough terrain and the small size

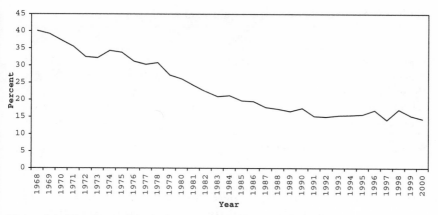

Figure 3.1. The share of Agriculture in GNP, 1980–2000 (in %).
Source: SIS, various issues.

of land holdings, however, wooden plows and hoes are still used extensively.

Another widely used indicator of agricultural modernization is the data on nitrogen, phosphorus, and potash-based fertilizer use. In the 1990–99 period, the proportion of fertilized area to total cultivated area increased to over 80 percent (SIS 1997, 114–15). Even though domestic fertilizer production doubled in the 1980–99 period, imports of fertilizers increased more than sixfold, presumably benefiting mostly the larger farm holders who can afford them.

Two factors played a major role in the slow pace of the introduction of modern agricultural technology: the small size of land holdings and the scarcity of human capital in rural areas.

Land holdings have traditionally been small in Turkey. According to Tunali: "the most striking feature of Turkish agriculture is the predominance of small, commercial farms that use family labor" (1993, 68). Keyder (1983, 130) refers to this structure as the parcellary mode of production. The 1980 and 1991 census data on agriculture support these observations (SIS 1992 and 1999). In 1980, 81.7 percent of holdings were ten hectares or less, using 40.96 percent of the total agricultural land. The relevant figures for 1991 were 85 and 42 percent, respectively. In fact, the majority of the farm holdings are smaller than five hectares. In 1980, 61 percent of farms smaller than five hectares occupied 20 percent of the total agricultural area. In 1991, their share increased to 23 percent. In the same time period, however, the share of large holdings more than doubled. From 1980–91, the share of

Table 3.1. Selected Agricultural Equipment and Machinery

	1980	1990	1999
Wooden plow	953292	500834	178052
Walking plow	804588	561024	308824
Horse drawn hoe	12899	7329	8851
Fertilizer distributor	74161	175073	287503
Four wheel tractors	435268	689343	915864

Source: SIS 1983, 236 and 1999, 311.

farms larger than 20 hectares increased from 6 to 14 percent. At the same time, single plot farms of the same size rose from 9 percent to almost 15 percent. Even though the agricultural sector is still mostly characterized by small-scale holdings there has been a rapid increase in the number of large farms, facilitated by mechanization and the availability of a wide variety of yield-increasing pesticides and fertilizers.

The limited availability of human capital in rural Turkey is reflected by the high rural illiteracy rates. In 1980, the rural illiteracy rate was a staggering 47 percent. In the following one and a half decades it was brought down to 30 percent. Even though this achievement can be considered significant in absolute terms, the scarcity of human capital in the agricultural sector remains a main bottleneck for the growth of agricultural productivity.

The yield rates in agriculture, that is, land productivity, in the last twenty years remained either constant or, at best, showed marginal changes. Table 3.2 gives the yields for selected agricultural commodities, which have a relatively high share in total agricultural production and/or in total agricultural exports.

Cereals have been one of Turkey's traditional agricultural commodities, but from 1980 to 1997, with the exception of maize, cereals displayed only marginal yield increases. Pulses and oil seeds and industrial crops exhibited effectively unchanged yields. The juxtaposition of this data to that of area sown, in Table 3.3, reveals the extent of the stagnation in the agricultural sector. Overall, the area sown remained unchanged, if not decreased, for most of the agricultural commodities. These two tables together provide a clear profile of the agricultural sector. The first characteristic is chronic stagnation in cereal production resulting from low productivity with no significant increases in area sown. The second characteristic is the shift away

Table 3.2. Yield of Selected Agricultural Produce (kg/hectare)

Cereals	1980	1985	1990	1999
Wheat	1829	1839	2116	1919
Rye	1186	1550	1519	1664
Barley	1893	1949	2179	2120
Oats	1802	1883	1972	1883
Maize	2127	3353	4078	4434
Rice	2750	2710	2604	3138
Pulses				
Broad Beans	1733	1738	1875	1857
Dry Beans	1447	1133	1229	1362
Lentils	1021	1072	934	735
Chick Peas	1146	1033	966	896
Oil Seeds				
Sunflower	1326	1245	1201	1597
Cotton Seed	1245	1256	1633	1798
Soybeans	1031	2076	2189	2750
Sesame	578	514	459	549
Groundnuts	2300	2783	2625	2679
Opium Seed	796	573	571	570
Industrial Crops				
Cotton	778	785	1021	1229
Sugar Beet	32493	30486	36819	38305
Tobacco	932	964	924	966

Source: SIS, various issues.

from traditional crops. Over time the relative importance of cereals decreased and that of industrial crops and oil seeds increased. In addition, fruit orchards and vegetable gardens expanded their share significantly. Figure 3.2 shows the increase in the area sown for orchards and vegetable gardens. The area sown for both vegetable and fruits steadily grew in the 1980s, with fruit orchards increasing faster than vegetable gardens. In both cases, the area sown fluctuated less in the 1980–97 period, implying a more stable income source for the farmers (Table 3.4). In contrast, the growth rate of the crop area sown dropped marginally, from .69 percent in 1970–79 to .63 percent in 1980–97.

Table 3.3. Area Sown of Selected Agricultural Produce (in thousand hectares).

Cereals	1980	1985	1990	1999
Wheat	9020	9350	9450	9380
Rye	443	240	158	140
Barley	2800	3350	3350	3650
Oats	220	167	137	154
Maize	585	567	515	518
Rice	75	62	53	65
Pulses				
Broad Beans	31	42	40	21
Dry Beans	110	150	171	174
Lentils	175	597	906	517
Chick Peas	200	399	890	625
Oil Seeds				
Sunflower	445	643	716	595
Cotton Seed	612	660	641	731
Soybeans	3	603	162	24
Sesame	45	88	85	51
Groundnuts	19	21	24	28
Opium Seed	19	5	9	55
Industrial Crops				
Cotton	672	660	641	731
Sugar Beet	269	323	380	440
Tobacco	323	177	320	260

Source: SIS, various issues.

According to SIS data (1993, 219–21; 1999, 287–91), total vegetable production rose by 7 million tons in 1980–99. In the same time period, production of root, bulb, and tuberous vegetables increased by almost 132 percent and that of fruit-bearing vegetables by about 58 percent. The leafy and leguminous vegetables showed only a marginal increase.

Regarding fruit production, citrus fruits and figs and apricots increased their shares significantly. For instance, grapefruit production jumped about threefold and tangerine production twofold in the 1980–97 period. Similarly to these traditional export fruits, hazelnuts continued to lead nut production as the main export nut of Turkey.

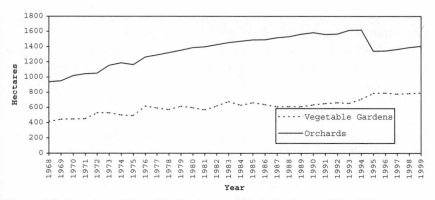

Figure 3.2. Area Sown: Vegetable Gardens and Fruit Orchards, 1968–1999
Source: SIS, various issues.

Another area in agriculture not mentioned so far is husbandry. Overall, husbandry has stagnated since the 1980s, predominantly as a result of the rise in net emigration in eastern and southeastern Turkey. The sharp drop in the number of cattle and sheep raised reduced meat production. For example, the stock of 42.5 million sheep in 1985 shrank by almost a quarter to 30 million in 1997. These developments led to meat imports to satisfy the protein-rich Turkish diet.

PUBLIC POLICY IN AGRICULTURE

Even though the shifts in the agricultural sector have not entirely resulted from domestic developments in the economy, those developments played a major role in the decline of the agricultural sector.

Table 3.4. Mean and Standard Deviation (SD) of Area Sown, 1970–79 and 1980–99

	Crops		Vegetable Gardens		Orchards	
	1970–79	1980–97	1970–79	1980–97	1970–79	1980–97
Mean	16091.42	18182.00	517.42	660.11	1144.42	1483.94
SD	866.95	361.01	70.43	65.28	143.38	–91.81

Source: Calculated from SIS, various issues.

Public policy choices dictated by the adjustment programs were prominent causes of the agricultural transformation.

The 1980 adjustment program hit the agricultural sector directly by forcing drastic changes in agricultural policies (see Cakmak et al. 1996). The drive to curb budget deficits affected agricultural credits and support prices. Drought and political pressure, however, rendered these policies unsustainable in the long run. In 1993, as part of the new stabilization program, government agricultural support purchases became limited to cereals, sugar beets, and tobacco, and the agricultural support price system was curbed significantly. Consequently, the agricultural sector went through a new adjustment phase. Olive production decreased substantially as a result of the cut in olive groves and trees. Some non-export fruit orchards and vineyards fell victim to the new agricultural regime as well.

As a result, Turkish agriculture fell short of providing sufficient food to the 19 million or so additional people that raised the Turkish population from 44 million to almost 64 million in 1997.

Agricultural credit and pricing policies are partially to be blamed for the poor performance of agriculture. The stop-and-go approach regarding agricultural credits and the support price system has failed to provide farmers with a consistent signal regarding agricultural markets. The behavior of agricultural credits is shown in Figure 3.3. The effort to control the expansion of agricultural credit in the 1980–88 period was relaxed in the 1990s, mainly as a result of political pressure, leading to a credit explosion in 1994. In addition, there was a shift in

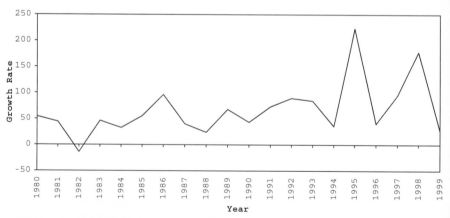

Figure 3.3. Growth Rate of Total Agricultural Credit
Source: SIS, various issues.

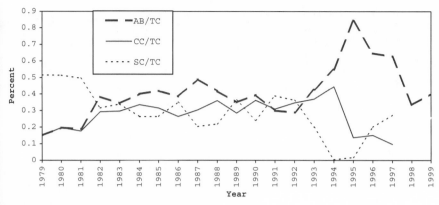

Figure 3.4. Agricultural Credits by Type
Source: SIS, various issues.

the composition of agricultural loans (Figure 3.4). The share of agricultural bank loans, AB, in total new loans, TC, decreased. The shares of credit cooperatives, CC/TC, and sales cooperatives and unions, SC/TC, increased by more than the decrease in the bank loans. Hence, after a sharp decline immediately following the inception of the 1980 stabilization program, financial resources were shifted from bank to nonbank agricultural finance institutions enabling the authorities to increase the total credit steadily, especially after 1988. The average growth rate of total agricultural credit in 1980–89 was negative 6.3 percent. It rose to about 12 percent in 1990–98.

A similar trend can be found in the support price system. The stop-and-go approach to controlling prices paid to farmers is displayed in Figures 3.5a through 3.5d. The figures show the percentage changes in the prices received by the farmers for six different cereals as well as for fruits and industrial crops. In all categories, the 1980–83 price decreases were relaxed in the mid-1980s and replaced by sharp price rises in the 1990s. An almost identical trend is seen in Figures 3.6 and 3.7, in prices received by nut and oil seed farmers.

In 1994, the OECD secretariat conducted an extensive study of the Turkish agricultural support scheme. The secretariat's estimates show that the producer subsidy equivalents of support prices (PSE calculates the transfer by consumers and taxpayers to agricultural producers) have increased in the 1990s. In other words, the authorities have continued to support agricultural prices to stabilize agricultural incomes: "However, in the three year period 1991–93, total

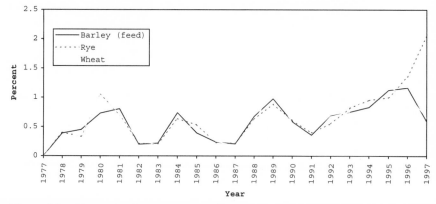

Figure 3.5a. Change in Cereal prices (in %)
Source: SIS, various issues.

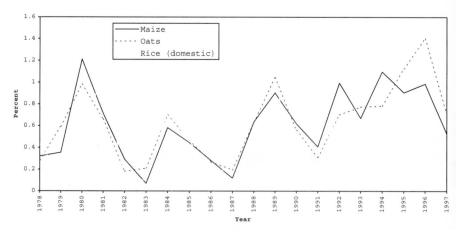

Figure 3.5b. Change in Cereal Prices (in %)
Source: SIS, various issues.

support is estimated to have risen around 40 percent, double the rate of the 1979–81 period and close to the OECD average. Thus, at a very aggregate level, the thrust of Turkish agricultural policy over the last several years has been to raise support levels significantly" (OECD Economic Survey 1994, 75).

Support prices provide the bulk of farm assistance in Turkey. The attractiveness of this scheme over the alternatives (for example, direct income payments) is that it is relatively easy to implement and

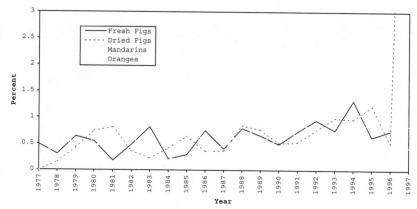

Figure 3.5c. Change in Fruit Prices (in %)
Source: SIS, various issues.

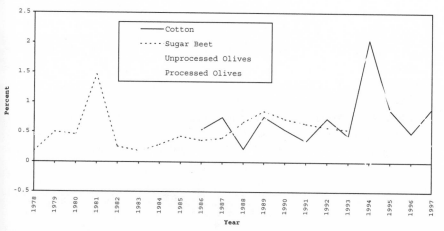

Figure 3.5d. Change in Industrial Crop Prices (in %)
Source: SIS, various issues.

has historically proved politically rewarding. The downside of the policy is that the three main SEEs in the agricultural sector—the Turkish Grain Board (TMO), Turkish Sugar Factories Incorporated (TSFAS), and the General Directorate for Tobacco and Tobacco Products, Salt, and Alcohol Industry (TEKEL), which set the relevant support prices—make up about half of the total SEE deficit.

Theoretically, support price schemes are inefficient, wasteful, costly, and potentially inflationary. Nevertheless, as the OECD re-

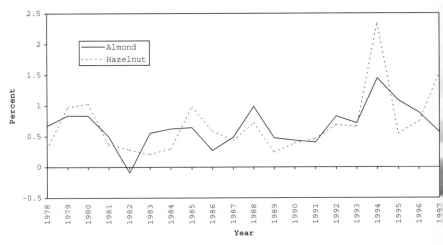

Figure 3.6. Change in Nut Prices (in %)
Source: SIS, various issues.

port shows, they were and still are in effect in industrial OECD countries as well. Only in 1998, in an effort to open up the agro-food sector to competition, did the ministers of agriculture of OECD countries agree on a set of shared agricultural goals. These goals cover a wide range, from rendering the sector responsive to market forces to guaranteeing that the sector contributes to food security "at the national and global levels" (OECD 1999a, 118). Turkey has been

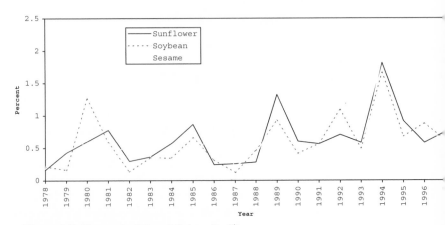

Figure 3.7. Change in Oilseed Prices (in %)
Source: SIS, various issues.

slow in adopting the operational criteria agreed upon at the 1998 meeting.

Whether made by the OECD, IMF, or the World Bank, policy recommendations regarding Turkish agriculture are strikingly similar: abolish the support price schemes, privatize the agricultural SEEs, and integrate agriculture into the world trading system to provide access to safer and cheaper food. OECD maintains: "Implementing these reforms should bring significant benefits relatively quickly to the Turkish consumers and taxpayers. If consumers were able to obtain food at world prices they would immediately experience a rise in effective income" (OECD Economic Survey 1999, 119). These benefits also would spread to the fiscal area in the form of budgetary savings that could be spent on, for instance, education and health. Furthermore, OECD echoes the standard IMF cry: "Loss-making state economic enterprises managing the market support schemes of the agricultural sector would no longer be necessary and could be closed, while Ziraat [Agriculture] Bank could concentrate on developing its financial intermediation skills rather than spending its efforts administering government subsidies. And ultimately the farming sector would gain because it would receive clearer signals about what to produce and the whole sector would become more efficient" (OECD Economic Survey 1999, 120).

This simplistically happy scenario would indeed carry certain adjustment costs. Currently about 45 percent of the total labor force employed in the agricultural sector would be subject to tectonic shifts the adjustment process would bring along. Unemployment and poverty would strike the already economically disadvantaged in the agricultural sector, increasing the urban-rural income gap.

Similarly, the Memorandum on Economic Policies dated June 26, 1998 and submitted to the IMF argued that agricultural support prices should be adjusted in line with the targeted inflation, and that interest rates on Ziraat Bank's agricultural loans be kept at least equal to the bank's average cost of funds to minimize their impact on the budget deficit (T.C. Basbakanlik Hazine Dairesi 1998). The first reference to the "rationalization" of agriculture first appeared in the September 29, 1999 Letter of Intent. In the name of rationalization the LoI proposed to eliminate the agricultural support price scheme by the end of 2002 and to replace it with the aforementioned direct income support system: "Present agricultural support policies are not the most cost effective way of providing support to poor farmers. They distort resource allocation by distorting market price signals, tend to benefit rich farmers more than the poor ones, and lack coherence given the fragmentation of the policy making process in this field among several ministries and public institutions. Above all, they have become quite onerous to the taxpayers with an average cost of about three percent of GNP in recent years. The medium-term objective of our reform programs [is] to phase out existing support policies and replace them with a direct income support system targeted to poor farmers" (LoI, September 29, 1999, 10).

Even though a direct income support system targeting the poor farmers is less welfare-reducing than the support price system, because the direct income scheme targets the individual farmer, the incomplete and unreliable farmer registration system in Turkey could pose an obstacle in reaching the needy farmers. It would be premature to talk about the effects of the direct support system, since it is not yet in place. In reality, in spite of the lip service to eliminate the support prices, achievements in this sphere have been negligible. There is also some doubt about the evidence that the support programs add up to 3 percent of GNP. There are conflicting reports in the literature regarding this cost figure. Turkish State Planning Organization estimates have consistently been lower than the Treasury's estimates (Oyan 2001, 23–24). Even the IMF recognizes that "at lower than 2 percent of GNP in the last three years, the primary fiscal cost of agricultural support policies in Turkey is lower than has generally been thought" (IMF 2000a, 72). In the meantime, insisting on limiting support price increases to the overly optimistic and unrealized low inflation targets inevitably invites skepticism about the effectiveness of the proposed agricultural reforms. Further damage may well result from the December 1999 LoI, which imposed the Chicago Board of Trade price for cereals (USA2HRW) as the world price of cereal: "The support price for cereals in 2000 will be set such that the spread between support prices and the projected world market price is no more than 35 percent of the projected c.i.f. world price, and reduced further in 2001 (to 20 percent)" (LoI, December 9, 1999, 10). The Chicago Board of Trade prices are predominantly affected by surplus cereal production in the United States. By imposing the US supply price on the Turkish farmers, the IMF has inadvertently condemned them to dependency by rendering them noncompetitive in domestic and foreign markets.

In the December 2000 letter of intent, authorities continued their promise to reform the agricultural sector and to phase out the indirect support policies and reduce involvement of the state in the production and marketing of agricultural products, thus leading "to a rapid privatization of the SEEs involved in this area" (LoI, December 18, 2000, 10). By mid-December 2000, the Parliament approved legislation that granted autonomy to the agricultural sales cooperatives and the cooperative unions (ASCUs) to facilitate the opening up of the agricultural sector: "in order to contain the cost of this transitional arrangement, and to encourage efficient, market-driven restructuring, the ASCUs will only be granted budgetary funds upon acceptance by the restructuring board (or, until it becomes operational, the Treasury and the Ministry of Industry and Trade acting on its behalf) of a business plan based on realistic market determined prices, and purchased volumes no greater than what can be expected to be sold, within a total operating and investment budget not exceeding their own funds plus the 2000 budget allocation from the government" (LoI, June 22, 2002).

The quote is telling in several respects. It shows once again that the Treasury is sidelining the "liberalization-unfriendly" Ministry of Agriculture on issues of importance to agriculture, and that the farmers are more and more left to the mercy of the markets without the safety net the state provides for dealing with the uncertainties of the agricultural sector. In addition, the removal of the state in the production and distribution of agricultural output would render it politically easy to privatize the SEEs in the sector: "The reform strategy for the tobacco sector and the restructuring of TEKEL, one of the main components in our agricultural policy reform and in our privatization drive, is being strengthened. We will transfer the state monopoly agency (TEKEL) to the Privatization agency (PA), instead of transforming only its tobacco processing units. To this end, a law, which would also reform the tobacco sector and phase out support purchases of tobacco, will be enacted by end-February 2001" (LoI, January 30, 2001). These words come not from the spokesperson for Reynolds, Rothman, or Seagram Corporation. The statement is quoted from the January 2001 letter of intent surrendering the tobacco and alcoholic beverage industries to the multinationals, which are facing an ever-increasing regulatory environment and profit loss in their home industrial countries. TEKEL has been earmarked for complete privatization by the end of 2002, and its monopoly on alcoholic beverages was virtually eliminated by mid-2001 with Raki, the Turkish national drink, being allowed to be produced privately. The June 2001 tobacco law, which was delayed because of political opposition and could only be brought to the Parliament after the resignation of the Privatization Minister Yalova, not only "rationalized" the tobacco production but also allowed companies that produce more than 2 billion cigarettes annually in Turkey to import and price a similar range of products (Essential Action 2001). Thus these companies also secured a large Turkish market for their products manufactured elsewhere. In the meantime a presidential veto once again delayed the privatization of TEKEL until 2002. The Treasury and Kemal Dervis, the minister of the economy, did not yield and announced that successful privatization needs to be preceded by major operational restructuring, "which we are determined to undertake in close cooperation with the World Bank" (LoI, January 28, 2002, 13). The determination to privatize TEKEL and other SEEs at all costs does invite questions, especially since letters of intent repeatedly state that subsidies to fertilizer, pesticides, and other agricultural inputs would remain in place, in spite of the fact that these subsidies predominantly benefit large and relatively rich farmers and foreign companies producing in and/or importing them to Turkey.

Finally, in his May 3, 2001 letter of intent (2001, 25), Kemal Dervis repeated the same promises of capping the support price increases at the targeted inflation rate, reducing cereal support purchases, reducing the excess cereal stocks, and privatizing the SEEs. Similarly, the focus of the May 3, 2001 memorandum on economic policies has been support prices regarding cereals, wheat in particular. In both cases the policy blueprint recommends keeping support price increases not just at but below the targeted inflation rate, and capping the price of wheat at no more than 20 percent above the world price as determined by the Chicago Board of Trade. Thus, cereal prices are being targeted persistently in an effort to replace domestic production by imports from the industrialized OECD countries. This misguided policy would increase Turkish dependency in agriculture and render it more vulnerable to exogenous shocks. The subordination of the agricultural sector to the urban-industrial sector, and the resulting high urbanization, would only aggravate the social, political, and economic problems facing both sectors. The costs associated with these problems unfortunately seem not to enter the cost-benefit calculations in liberalization and privatization programs.

The volatility of the agricultural economy, its low labor and land productivity, and the anti-agriculture bias inherent in the post–1980 stabilization program, all inevitably affected the relative distribution of income in the economy, as shown in Table 3.5, which displays the quintile distribution of income in Turkey. In spite of the marginal in-

Table 3.5. Income Distribution in Turkey, 1987 and 1994

	Total		Urban		Rural	
	1987	1994	1987	1997	1987	1997
1st quintile	5.2	4.9	5.4	4.8	5.2	5.6
2nd quintile	9.6	8.6	9.3	8.2	10.0	10.1
3rd quintile	14.1	12.6	13.6	11.9	15.0	14.8
4th quintile	21.2	19.0	20.7	17.9	22.0	21.8
5th quintile	49.9	54.9	50.9	57.2	47.8	47.7

Source: SIS 1987:278 and Kongar 1995:637.

crease in the income share of the bottom quintile in 1994, rural average income per household was 42 percent lower than the corresponding urban income. In 1987, this ratio was 24 percent (Cakmak 1998, 12). The gap is most likely the result of the pro-industry bias of the stabilization program. In spite of the seemingly deliberate public policy to transfer resources into agriculture, the sector has not been able to maintain its share in the economy. As the data on agricultural prices and credits reveal, public policy in the 1980s was more obedient to the requirements of the stabilization and liberalization program and had a counter-agriculture and pro-industry bias. Accordingly, the agricultural sector was harmed. Political pressure in the early 1990s caused the governments to revert to their old paternalistic behavior, with agricultural credits and prices rising. Nevertheless, the agricultural sector was already hit hard and had started to shrink.

Other recent agricultural reform attempts include restructuring the agricultural credit markets, a transition to alternative crops, the design and implementation of a direct agricultural income support system, privatization of state-owned agricultural enterprises, and additional reforms to manage agriculture more efficiently. These reform proposals are indeed an attempt to open up the agricultural sector to market forces. In an era of internationalization of economic activity, liberalization of an economic sector inevitably implies that that sector is affected and shaped by the world markets.

INTERNATIONAL DIVISION OF LABOR IN AGRICULTURE

These agricultural difficulties under economic liberalization are not unique to Turkey. Barkin (1983 and 1987), Sanderson (1985),

Reynolds et al. (1993), Bryceson (1997), Rigg and Nattapoolwat (2001) have written extensively on the agricultural problems in Mexico, Puerto Rico, Dominican Republic, Africa, and Thailand. David et al. (2000) analyzed how economic liberalization has affected agriculture in Latin America, in general and in Brazil, Chile, and Mexico in particular. They claim that the privatization of agricultural activity has created vacuums that have not been filled by the private sector. The authors summarize the structural changes in Latin American agriculture, whereby export agriculture, predominantly oil seeds, fruits, and vegetables have flourished at the expense of traditional products like roots and tubers. They also point out that in the three case studies on Brazil, Mexico, and Chile, small farmers have disproportionately borne the costs of privatization: "They [small farmers] usually have insufficient human and other capital to move into other significantly more productive activities, either in their own locality or through migration. Given the sheer magnitude of their numbers in most countries of the region, it is hard to see how policy makers could ignore them or pretend to tackle the issue through social programs alone. Clearly, a balance has to be struck between social programs sustainable in a budgetary sense, and productivity enhancing programs, taking into account possible market and government failures as well as civil society at large" (David et al. 2000, 1,673–74).

In Turkey, as in Latin America, the deliberate policy of transferring income from rural to urban-industrial sectors to promote manufactured good exports seems to have reached its limits. Deflationary policies have had significant adverse effects on investment and lowered the output growth. With a large proportion of the labor force still in agriculture, authorities have little choice but to take extensive, integrated measures to raise overall agricultural productivity, which would eventually increase final demand in the economy. If they also supplement these with a national food policy, agriculture in developing countries, including Turkey, may reach a self-sustaining growth path.

As already mentioned at the beginning of this chapter, the contemporary world food system promotes the international division of labor in agriculture in line with the principle of comparative advantage, whereby industrial countries (notably the United States and the European Union) specialize in relatively capital- and technology-intensive grain and cereal production, and developing countries in relatively labor-intensive fruit and vegetable production (Friedmann 1991; Cochrane and Runge 1992).

The systematic efforts to shape the world food system date back to the post–World War II Marshall Plan and Public Law 480 (Food for Peace Program), which helped the United States rid itself of the grain surplus in the postwar years. At the same time, these efforts helped develop future export markets for US agricultural products. McMichael (1996, 57–75, 100–110) discusses extensively the role of the United States in the division of labor in the world agricultural system. Acker summarizes the effects of the Food for Peace Program: "Food aid programs provide an opportunity to empty our granaries, and our warehouses, build taste preferences for US commodities, and build purchasing power for future commercial sales of US agricultural commodities. According to a recent study, former recipients of US food aid are now the largest commercial purchasers of American farm products" (1989, 165).

In building the world food system, the West has used its political leverage and subsidized its agricultural sector substantially in the mid-1970s and early-1980s and successfully brought world grain prices down, influencing the structure of agriculture in developing countries (McMichael 1996, 57–75). The aggregate world food price index decreased from 1973 to 1979, and again later, from 1981 to 1988 (IMF 2001d, 184–87). A similar trend also occurred in wheat, maize, and other individual grain prices. Accordingly, this change in the relative price of agricultural commodities had an effect on the composition of the agricultural sector in developing countries, forcing them away from grain to fruit and vegetable production. McMichael describes this world food system as one where the "US has assumed a global 'breadbasket of the world' strategy and sought to institutionalize its corporate 'food power' via the current free trade regime" (2000, 127). Thompson and Cowan, for instance, show that "the key dimension of current Asian agro-food system restructuring [is]: Displacement of long-standing imperatives of national food self-sufficiency by regional and global import regimes centered around agro-food transnationals" (2000, 401–7). The international division of labor paradigm is in place in Latin America, Asia, Turkey, and elsewhere in countries restructuring their agriculture under the supervision of the IMF, World Bank, and WTO.

A concomitant link in the chain of changes in the world agricultural structure is multinational agrochemical corporations' penetration into the developing countries. Agrobusinesses are generally engaged in the provision of relatively inexpensive chemical fertilizers and pesticides, hybrid seeds, and ultimately genetically modified crops. The new world agricultural order helps agrobusinesses enter the developing countries because vegetable and fruit production reduces soil protection, increasing the need for fertilizers and insecticides. Agrobusinesses claim that the changes they introduce lead to cheaper and safer food supplies, produced in an ecologically friendly environment. The WTO and recently the United Nations joined the bandwagon of international organizations that echo the voice of the agrobusinesses. Critics of agro-business involvement in agriculture argue that it favors large farmers; they also raise questions concerning public health, the environment, and the desirability of a homogenous food supply. The *New York Times* on July 8, 2001 ran a page-five article on the United Nations report claiming that genetically engineered food would eradicate hunger in poor countries (*New York Times* 2001). The same day, the *Times'* magazine section featured a lengthy article on child poverty and hunger in the United States (*New York Times Magazine* 2001). None of its editors bothered addressing the issues concerning the distribution of excess food stocks. Clearly the availability of food in one of the world's richest countries is not the cause of child hunger. As Lane puts it: "It is not the overall availability of food and its nutrients in the United States that is considered a problem. It is its distribution and use" (1995, 1,096).

In general, Turkey was no exception to the changes that affected world agriculture. As shown earlier, the country has been shifted from grain production to vegetable and fruit production. Agribusiness has also entered Turkish agriculture. Conagra, Inc., Pharmacia and Upjohn, Procter & Gamble Co., and Novartis are actively engaged in Turkish agriculture, producing and/or importing fertilizers, herbicides, and insecticides, totaling about 14 percent of total imports. Fortunately, genetically modified organisms (GMO), on the other hand, have not fully penetrated the agricultural sector, at least for the time being. The Ministry of Agriculture has been resisting imports of agricultural products unless they are certified GMO-free because of the fear that GMO products pose unknown risks regarding human and animal health and the environment. The ministry also requires importers to obtain sanitary certifications and lab results on certain food ingredients to keep imports GMO-free. Further, in spite of the fact that insecticide applications are common and frequent enough to affect the environment adversely, production of organic foods is on the rise in Turkey (US Department of Agriculture 2000, 1).

Another agriculture-related development taking place in Turkey is the result of increasing income and its effects on lifestyles, tastes, and consumption patterns. Families eat more and more outside their homes, especially at fast-food restaurants, like McDonald's, KFC, and Burger King (Sirtioglu 2002, 1–2). These fast food chains rely on imports of products to secure quality, and as the number of their franchises increases, it is likely that they will import more and more necessary ingredients. In addition to the impact on trade balance, a potentially more undesirable effect could be on the diet and tastes of individuals. In the way the Marshall Plan affected diet in developing countries in favor of cash crops, the fast-food industry reinforces dietary changes in favor of the industrial agrobusinesses.

Let us now turn to the trade effects of these changes. If the world food system hypothesis has any merit, agricultural trade flows between industrial and developing countries would be expected to reflect it. If we take the agricultural trade between Turkey and the United States as a case study, we would expect the United States to have a deficit in the labor-intensive vegetable and fruit trade, and Turkey to have a deficit in the relatively capital-intensive grain and feed trade. Table 3.6 lists the US trade position regarding Turkey in several agricultural categories. The distribution of the trade balance in the table follows the dictum of the world food system. The United States has a comparative advantage and exports relatively more cap-

Table 3.6. U.S. Trade Position with Turkey, Selected Agricultural Commodities, 1980–99

Agricultural Commodity	Trade Position
Fruit Juices	deficit
Fresh/frozen fruit	deficit
Fruits—prep/pres	deficit
Grains and feeds	surplus
Fertilizers	surplus
Insecticides	surplus
Oil Seeds	surplus
Olives	deficit
Pistachio Nuts	deficit
Soybean and soybean oil	surplus
Tobacco	deficit
Vegetables—fresh/frozen	deficit
Vegetables—prep/pres	deficit
Wheat, unmilled	surplus

Source: US Department of Agriculture Economic Research Service, 2000.

ital-intensive and high value-added agricultural commodities, such as fertilizers, wheat, soybeans, whereas Turkey's comparative advantage and exports come from relatively more labor-intensive and low value-added agricultural goods like fruit, olives, and vegetables. Sarigedik in a report prepared for the USDA reinforces the U.S.–Turkey trade pattern in agriculture: "As a result of increasing demand for higher quality combined with limited land resources and crop quality improvements, Turkey is expected to remain a significant long-term wheat importer. In addition, Turkey is also expected to remain a long-term rice and corn importer. The U.S. is well positioned to meet the grain demand for constant quality and value . . . GSM-102 credit guarantee programs also remain an important marketing tool for U.S. wheat, feed grains, and rice. . . . Turkey used to be a major producing and exporting country for pulses. But, production decreased significantly. The U.S. may become a major supplier" (2002, 7–8).

At first sight, one could argue that this trade pattern supports the comparative advantage principle. The capital-intensive country, the United States, is producing and exporting capital-intensive agricultural produce, and labor-intensive Turkey is producing and exporting labor-intensive vegetables and fruits. However, the comparative advantage theory assumes free trade and the United States trade policy is laden with extensive protection of the agricultural sector. It is very hard to use the comparative advantage argument in this protective environment.

CONCLUSIONS

Economic liberalization has taken its toll on Turkish agriculture. Low world agricultural prices, the reduction in subsidies and support prices, aggressive US and EU policies to restructure the world agricultural system, and anti-agricultural bias in the stabilization programs have all contributed to the decline of the agricultural sector, leading to the worsening off of those whose livelihood depends on agriculture. The recent push by the WTO to implement the Uruguay Round Agreement on Agriculture to reduce "trade distortions" could aggravate the short-term and medium-term problems of the agricultural sectors in Turkey and other developing countries. This scenario is especially likely if industrial countries maintain their agricultural protections, which deny developing countries access to export markets (see Hoekman and Anderson 2000, 179). The agricultural policy recommendations from the UN World Summit on Sustainable Development in Johannesburg in August 2002 show that the United Nations is more objective and democratic than the IMF/World Bank and the WTO, and not as subservient to the wishes of the United States and other industrial countries (United Nations 2002). Maybe it is time to reorganize the IMF/World Bank and the WTO under the auspices of the UN. After all, in one form or another, they are fossil remnants of the Bretton Woods. It is time for change.

Problems specific to Turkey are in abundance. One of the domestic reasons for the decline in agriculture's share in the economy is the net emigration from eastern and southeastern Turkey. Animal farming has been especially hurt by these declines in population. Unless this situation is reversed by efforts to repopulate these regions, there will be limited opportunities for a credible agricultural policy reform. The Southeastern Anatolian Project (GAP) promises to bring economic vitality to the area. However, to realize its potential, a permanent peace with the Kurdish people in the region is essential. Also needed is a full-fledged rural development program, led by the state and independent NGOs with an emphasis on education and other policies directed at small farmers, to complement the GAP and to reinhabit the region. This program would meet the basic needs of the peoples in the region and also provide them with cultural, social, and political freedom. Such rural development plans would render agriculture in the region self-supportive and self-sustaining. Within this program, provision of property rights should have priority. In eastern provinces, as elsewhere in Anatolia, land ownership may not be a registered and legally well-documented asset. The provision of legal entitlement to land is one of the first steps in mobilizing capital, so essential for rural development. Hernando de Soto (2000) in his recent book, *The Mystery of Capital,* discusses extensively how to "paperize" these assets, and explains the government's role in this process. Legal property ownership would enable the farmers' use of their assets as collateral in accessing the formal capital markets and would help them participate in the formal economy as productive agents.

Provision of property ownership and access to credit markets alone would not suffice to overcome problems stemming from the small size of farms in Turkey. Similarly, getting prices right, as the IMF and World Bank insist, is not the solution to the problems of farmers. Small farms not only constrain the modernization of agriculture but also limit farmers' access to information and to domestic and foreign markets. Turkey already has had extensive experience with agricultural cooperatives. They date back to the foundation of the Republic in 1923. A reemphasis on agricultural cooperatives, augmented by rational agricultural extension services and formal and informal educational institutions, would facilitate the introduction of debt-free seeds, modern methods and technology, and would enhance financial intermediation, storage, domestic and international marketing, and the distribution of the agricultural produce. The cooperatives would also empower the fragmented small farmers and contribute to their achieving self-sufficiency in agriculture. Programs involving technical assistance and agricultural extension services must also take into consideration that 40 to 45 percent of the labor force in agriculture is women. Hence, these initiatives should explicitly address women's needs, such as health care, education, and access to credit.

Small farmers lack the necessary economies of scale and the financial resources to take advantage of synthetic fertilizers and pesticides. The authorities could aid the farmers in using locally produced biopesticides and biofertilizers. Especially in the wake of European and US food scares, organic farming may provide a comparative advantage to the Turkish small farmers. Mechanization and use of fertilizers, herbicides, and insecticides deteriorate the soil. In addition, excessive irrigation and the use of agrochemical inputs may salinize and sterilize the soil, respectively. In order to reverse environmental damage and to support organic agricultural practices, authorities need to provide incentives to raise rural awareness regarding the merits of integrated crop rotation, pest management, composting, and soil conservation, to name a few. In order to provide leadership in organic farming, domestic and international NGOs can be mobilized. For instance, the Australian Conservation Foundation, a Melbourne-based Permaculture Global Assistance Network (PGAN), has helped the Cuban government introduce new organic rural and urban farming techniques that made Cuba self-sufficient regarding their food supply within a short time after the collapse of the Soviet Union (Tiller, 1996). These and similar measures would not only support environmentally sustainable agricultural practices but would also make Turkish agricultural products more competitive in the organic-friendly European export markets. In this regard, authorities need to keep in mind the risks importing grains from the United States might pose. Imported corn, wheat, and other grains may expose the domestic production to cross-pollination with genetically engineered U.S. varieties, as has happened in India and recently in Mexico. Even though Turkish laws ban planting genetically altered seeds, winds and farmers illegally planting seeds from imported grains can cause cross-pollination and introduce genetically engineered crops to Turkish agriculture.

The agricultural sector should be in the core of the Turkish development strategy and should have the top priority. The government should provide full support to agriculture to increase domestic food production to decrease Turkey's dependence on food imports. Agriculture is too important to be left to the whim of free markets. The livelihood of a large fraction of the population still derives from agriculture. The new economic model of industrialization ties the agricultural sector into the world food system that renders developing countries dependent on industrial countries. Modern agriculture, with its hybrid seeds and chemical inputs, incorporates agriculture into multinational agrobusiness (McMichael 2000, 137). But there are alternatives to this model. Elsewhere, the use of appropriate ecological technology by small- and medium-size farmers and an active role by the government have led to environmentally friendly agricultural practices and self-reliance in food production (Rosset 2000, 212). Turkish authorities should search for the alternatives suitable for the realities of the Turkish agriculture rather than rush to give in to the one-for-all prescriptions of the OECD, World Bank, IMF, and WTO.

4

Environment and Liberalization

IN THE POST-1980S PERIOD THE AVERAGE ANNUAL GROWTH RATE OF THE Turkish economy has hovered around 4.5 percent. This relatively rapid economic growth prompts an investigation of the effects of liberalization policies on the environmental sustainability. The lack of appropriate public policy to counter the effects of industrialization and liberalization, which promoted poverty and the growth of dirty industries, has contributed to environmental degradation. The first part of this chapter draws on the existing but limited data to describe the state of the environment in Turkey; it then discusses the impact of the rise in industrial output and trade on environmental quality, and analyzes the merits of the argument that dirty industries may have migrated from Europe to Turkey. Finally, short- and long-run policy recommendations targeting sustainable development are proposed.

THE STATE OF THE ENVIRONMENT

The relationship between economic growth and the quality of the environment has generally sparked controversy. The famous Kuznets curve argues that at low levels of income, income growth corresponds to an increase in environmental degradation. After a certain critical income level y^*, however, further increases in per capita income reduce environmental degradation. High income enables a country to afford either environmental cleanup costs in industry or the use of green and modern technology, or both. The inverted U-shaped Kuznets curve in Figure 4.1 captures this relationship between income growth and environmental quality. It is based on factual data for industrial countries where changes in the composition of aggregate output and technological progress over time may have contributed to the declining tail of the curve. In addition, a higher educational attainment level in such countries has raised environmental

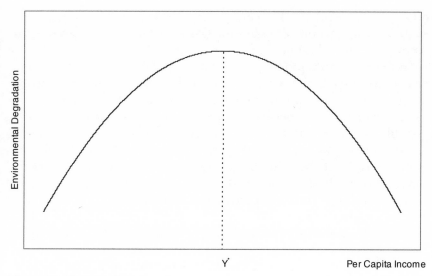

Figure 4.1. Kuznets Curve

awareness and led people to demand more pollution control and higher quality of life. Efforts to improve environmental quality have also been facilitated by the fall in population growth rates following economic development and growth. A Dasgupta and Maler (1995) study pointed out that an additional reason for the shape of the Kuznets curve is that the share of service industries in the economy rises as growth progresses and structural change takes place.

Developing countries, on the other hand, are mostly located along the rising tail of the curve, where the increase in environmental degradation exceeds the increase in per capita income as growth in per capita income rises. Several empirical studies have investigated the level of critical income, y^*, in Figure 4.1, to estimate the reflection point on the curve. For instance, Grossman and Krueger (1991) found that the critical level of the average per capita income in 1985 US dollars is about $5,000, above which urban pollution decreases.

A World Bank study (1992) refers to additional environment-related stylized facts, especially in urban areas: as per capita GDP rises, the share of population without safe drinking water and adequate sanitation diminishes, and similarly, so do urban concentrations of particulate matter and sulfur dioxide. These findings reinforce the Kuznets hypothesis relating rising incomes to improvements in the environment quality. According to the same study, though, the increase in per capita GDP creates an increase in per capita municipal waste and in carbon dioxide emissions, resulting from greater urbanization and a higher number of motor vehicles.

Similarly, Shafik and Bandyopadhyay (1992) have provided empirical evidence at the macroeconomic level as to how environmental quality changes with income. Their findings, which need to be regarded with caution because of data limitations, suggest that it is possible to grow out of environmental problems with economic growth as long as appropriate environmental and macroeconomic policies are implemented as well. The study is important, however, since it has emphasized the fact that the relationship between income growth and improvement in environmental quality is not automatic, as some might think.

Post-1980 growth in the Turkish economy has not yet reached a level at which economic growth would reduce environmental degradation. Thus, Turkey faces a trade-off between growth and environmental degradation for some time to come. The question, however, is how much further environmental conditions could deteriorate without drastically reducing the well-being of future generations— that is, at what point further growth would reduce environmental sustainability. In this context, environmental sustainability refers to the preservation of the physical and natural capital available for future generations (World Bank 1992, 8). In the case of Turkey, the problem is further aggravated by a high population growth rate. The current average annual population growth rate is still high, at 1.5 percent, even though it has slowed from 2.3 percent in the 1980s. At the current rate of 1.5 percent, the present population of 66 million would increase to 81 million in 2020 (World Resources Institute 2001). Even though the overall population density is still low, 85 persons per square km, the current high population growth would inevitably place an additional burden on economic resources and the environment, especially in regions that are destinations for high internal migration. In short, the distribution of population growth and of density has not been even. The Marmara, Aegean, and Mediterranean regions have grown disproportionately in relation to other regions in the country. Istanbul, for instance, had a population of 8 million in 1999 and a density of over 1,000 persons/km^2. Furthermore, the growth in urbanization is alarming. The percentage of the population living in urban areas has increased from 34 percent in 1965 to 61 percent in 1990 and to 64.7 percent in 1997 (SIS, various issues). As a result of their "ruralization" the urban industrial centers (for example, Istanbul, Izmit, Izmir, Adana, and Bursa) have suffered from significant socioeconomic and environmental effects. The rise in urban poverty and the need for housing, sanitation, schooling, health facilities and other services confront the authorities with extremely difficult challenges. The economic cost of delivering these needed services versus the political cost of preventing slums from growing is indeed not a pleasant choice for politicians. As already mentioned in chapter 3, the high urbanization rate has also taken its toll on the agricultural sector, causing environmental damage in the rural areas. The intensive use of pesticides and chemical fertilizers, on one hand, and the increasing poverty, on the other, have accelerated the rapid deterioration of the natural capital endowment in rural areas.

Reliable environmental data in Turkey are scarce. A systematic and consistent database has slowly begun to be compiled, only since the Ministry of Environment was founded in 1991. The following environmental profile of Turkey has been drawn using these available data.

Indicators of environmental quality focus on three natural resources: air, water, and land. Table 4.1 summarizes the relevant environmental indicators concerning these three natural resources. The available data show that the Turkish environmental record is mixed. Let us now turn to each of the natural resources individually.

Air Quality

High urbanization resulting from the pro-urban and anti-rural economic liberalization policies inevitably affected urban air quality adversely. According to the Turkish National Environmental Action Plan (1999, 29), "An average of 15 million residents of Turkey's major cities were exposed to particulates and SO_2 (sulphur dioxide) levels above WHO (World Health Organization) levels from 1990–96. If annual levels could achieve WHO standards, an estimated 3350 lives could have been saved in 1993 and there would have been approximately 5940 fewer hospital admissions for respiratory ailments."

In the 1990–97 period, total sulfur dioxide emissions increased by 28 percent and carbon dioxide emissions by 24 percent (SIS, 1998). Whereas carbon dioxide emissions in the world as a whole dropped between 1990 and 1995 from 4.08 to 3.92 tons per person, in Turkey they increased from 3.15 to 3.49 tons per person. Moreover, fuel-based carbon dioxide emission rose from 2.53 to 2.79 tons per person, by 10.3 percent.

Table 4.1. Indicators of Environmental Conditions

	1990	1996	% change
Air			
Nitrogen Oxide	275	497	81%
CO_2 Emissions (1000 Metric Tons)	143819	178342	24%
CO_2 Emissions Per Int'l $ GDP	554	474	14%
Water			
Annual Withdrawal (1997):			
Percent of Water Resources	18		
Per Capita (cubic mt)	560		
Sectoral Withdrawals (percent of total):			
Domestic	16%		
Industry	11%		
Agriculture	73%		
Marine, Freshwater Catches and Aquaculture Production (Percent Change 1985–87 to 1995–97):			
Marine	–13%		
Freshwater	19%		
Mollusk & Crustacean	59%		
Total Aquaculture Production	1005		
Average Annual Groundwater Withdrawals:			
Total (km^3)	20		
Percent of Annual Recharge (1995)	38%		
Per capita (1995) (hm^3)	114.1		
Per capita (2000)	300		
Annual Renewable Water Resources (cubic mt):	2943		
Population with Access to Safe Drinking Water, 1990–97:			
Rural	25%		
Urban	66%		
Total	49%		
Land	1987	1997	
Cropland (total hectares)	27927	29162	
Irrigated Land (Percent of total cropland)	12%	14%	

(*continued*)

Table 4.1. Indicators of Environmental Conditions (*continued*)

	1990	1996	% change
Average Annual Use (kg/hectare of cropland):			
Fertilizer	58	66	
Pesticides (1996 figure only)	1145	—	
Average Annual Production (Percent Change 1986–88 to 1996–98) Roundwood:			
Industrial	49.60%		
Wood Fuel	–20.10%		
Total	7%		
Wood Products:			
Wood Panels	150%		
Paper and Paperboard	68%		

Source: World Resources Institute 2001.

Even though there is not enough hard evidence to quantify its extent, in Turkey's large cities, though not in medium-size mid- and eastern Anatolian cities (for example, Erzurum, Diyarbakir, Kutahya, and Konya), the relatively recent switch from coal to natural gas as a domestic heating source has helped to reduce SO_2 and particulate matter concentrations. It should be borne in mind, however, those urban slums and households that cannot afford the cost of conversion still rely predominantly on coal, especially cheaper, highly polluting lignite coal.

Another major source of pollution in cities is motor vehicles. In the last ten years, the number of cars, vans, trucks, buses, and pickup trucks in Turkey has more than doubled. For example, the number of private passenger cars increased from 1.8 million in 1991 to 3.8 million in 1998 (SIS 1999, 400). At the same time, the composition of car consumption changed. Purchases of high-speed luxury cars increased significantly. The sales of Alfa Romeo, BMW, Land Rover, and other luxury status-symbol cars rose more than threefold (SIS 1999, 401–7). Consequently, gasoline consumption jumped in the same time period. In Turkey, leaded gasoline still constitutes over 90 percent of vehicle fuel use, and lead emission is a significant source of air pollution, particularly in large cities. The rising number of motor vehicles on the roads and the consequent heavy traffic have also contributed to noise pollution and, more importantly, to an increasing number of traffic accidents and deaths. According to the National Environment Action Plan, traffic noise in Istanbul in 1999 reached 10 to 25 dBA higher than the limits in other countries (1999, 35). According to the same source, there were 440,149 traffic accidents in 1998, with 4,935 dead and 114,552 injured. The statistics on traffic-accident related fatalities put Turkey among the top ten countries in the world.

A different way of looking at air quality is in terms of the emission of greenhouse gases; in Turkey these increased by 35 percent in 1990–97 (Table 4.2). Among the three major greenhouse gas categories, carbon dioxide (CO_2), methane (CH_4), and dinitrogen monoxide (N_2O). CO_2 constitutes 88.9 percent of the total emissions, followed by CH_4 (9.42 percent) and N_2O (1.65 percent). The two primary sources of carbon dioxide emissions are energy consumption (burning of fossil fuels) and industrial processes. The two other greenhouse gases come predominantly from burning agricultural waste. Unfortunately there are no data on an additional group of greenhouse gases, chlorofluorocarbons (CFCs) emitted by refrigerants. The worrisome aspect of the CO_2 emissions is that, unlike in other OECD countries, which are experiencing decreasing carbon dioxide emissions, in Turkey they have increased, from 3.15 tons/person in 1990 to 3.49 tons/person in 1995. The world emission figures, similar to those of the OECD, show a downward trend, dropping from 4.08 tons/person in 1990 to 3.92 in 1995. The alarming aspect of the relatively high emission figures in Turkey is that the annual emission of greenhouse gases is expected to double by 2020 as a result of projected high energy consumption and production to meet the needs of the industrial sector (National Environmental Action Plan 1998, 28). Already during 1987–97, the share of the industrial sector in energy consumption increased from 27.7 percent to 33.7 percent, with the share of the residential sector decreasing from 40 percent to 32 percent. Transportation (22.8 percent) and agriculture (5.3 percent) made up the remaining difference.

As can be seen, Turkey's energy balance is not very promising. According to the World Resources Institute (2001, 288), in spite of the significant increase in hydroelectric and geothermal energy production in recent years, the 54 percent increase in overall energy consumption has led in 1998 to a trade deficit in energy of 43.3 toe (tonnes equivalent), increasing Turkey's dependency on energy im-

Table 4.2. Greenhouse Gas Emissions, 1990–97

	1990	1991	1992	1993	1994	1995	1996	1997
Greenhouse Gas Emissions (mil. Tonnes)	200.72	207.42	214.97	225.91	222.51	241.81	262.49	271.18
Indexed, 1990=100	100	103.34	107.1	112.55	110.85	120.47	130.77	135.1
Per Capita Greenhouse Gas Emissions (tonnes)	3.55	3.63	3.71	3.84	3.73	3.99	4.27	4.34
Total Carbon Dioxide Emissions (mil. Tonnes)	17.97	182.69	188.49	198.79	197.46	211.3	231.35	241.15
Indexed, 1990=100	100	102.65	105.65	111.69	111.51	118.73	129.99	135.5
Per Capita Carbon Dioxide Emissions (tonnes)	3.15	3.2	3.2	3.38	3.32	3.49	3.76	3.86
Composition of Greenhouse Gas Emissions (%):								
CO_2	89	88	88	88	89	87	88	89
CH_4	11	11	10	10	10	10	10	9
N_2O	1	1	2	2	1	3	2	2

Source: SIS, various issues.

ports. The pro-industry bias in the liberalization policies has been instrumental in this increase in dependency.

Water Quality

Turkey is endowed generously with salt- and freshwater sources. It is surrounded by the Black Sea, the Aegean, and the Mediterranean, and has an inland sea, the Marmara, as well as over forty large natural lakes and more than twenty river basins and streams exceeding a total of 30,000 kms. In spite of this abundance, however, high withdrawal (Table 4.1), industrial and residential waste, and agricultural runoff have put these vast water resources at risk. Turkey's annual total freshwater withdrawal, 35.5 hm^3 in 1997, amounts to 560 cubic meters per person and constitutes 18 percent of freshwater resources. Agriculture's share of total withdrawal is 73 percent followed by those of residential and industrial use, 16 and 11 percent, respectively (World Resources Institute 2001, 276). Nevertheless, in the midst of this abundance of water, only 49 percent of the population had access to safe drinking water in 1990–97, 25 percent in the rural areas and 66 percent in the urban areas (Table 4.1). In the urban areas, those who live in the slums typically have no access to safe water.

Sewage statistics indicate a significantly worse situation and reveal serious potential environmental and health hazards. Even though around 65 percent of the population has access to sewage collection systems, only 6 percent are served by treated sewage facilities. Even today, the rural population overall has no access to any public sewage system (OECD Economic Survey 1992 and SIS 1999). In addition to the discharge of untreated sewage by households, industry has been a major contributor to wastewater pollution. In 1992, 69 percent of the wastewater and 58 percent of the sewage discharged by industry was not treated. In 1994, only 22 percent of manufacturing establishments either had their own or shared a wastewater treatment plant. Wood products, metal-manufacturing industries, and non-metallic mineral products, all rapidly growing manufacturing industries, had negligible wastewater treatment records, between .01 and 10 percent (SIS, 1999, 40–53). The two traditional major recipients of discharged wastewater have been streams and septic tanks, potentially affecting the underground water resources. Solid waste dumping has been further decreasing the quality of underground water. The average amount of per capita solid waste created in 1994 was 1.01 kg in the summer and 1.12 kg in the winter. Thirty-five percent of the municipal solid waste was disposed by dumping into rivers and 20 percent by burning in open areas. Other means of disposal included dumping into the sea and lakes, and burial. Pollution has been shifted from one area to another, but not reduced.

Hazardous waste disposal has also proved problematic in Turkey because of the lack of hazardous waste dumps or incineration facilities. The few existing facilities are either of substandard quality and do not function effectively, or are inefficient because of lax enforcement of existing rules and regulations. Domestic sources, such as medical and industrial facilities, have not been the only producers of hazardous materials. Foreign sources, the lack of public awareness, and local officials' lack of accountability have all contributed to domestic environmental problems.

In 1988, hundreds of barrels of toxic waste washed ashore on the Black Sea coast. Locals emptied the containers to use for food and rainwater storage. As a result, many people developed skin rashes and nausea. Investigation revealed that the barrels were contaminated with paint, benzene, and cellulose lacquer waste, as well as DDT and PCBs. Apparently, the barrels were being shipped from Italy to Bulgaria but somehow were dumped into the sea and found their way to the Turkish coast (Milliyet 2000). The incident has helped the public to pressure the Turkish authorities to ban the imports of industrial and hazardous waste for industrial fuel and storage. In spite of these efforts, however, several Western industrial countries continued contributing to environmental degradation in developing countries, typified by World Bank chief economist Lawrence L. Summers's 1991 internal memo arguing for the transfer of waste and dirty industries from industrial to developing countries, because developing countries were less polluted (Summers 1991).

In another episode in 1994, Eurogold, a multinational mining company, has been taken to Turkish courts by the inhabitants of the villages near Bergama, a town on the Western coast of Turkey, on charges that the company used cyanide leaching in its mining process, polluting the underground water resources and affecting human health. Even though the court decided against the Eurogold Company in 1997, the Turkish Ministry of Environment refused to implement the court order on the basis of a technicality. The case has recently been submitted to the European Human Rights Court in Strasbourg.

Hazardous waste from Western industrial countries enters Turkey in different forms. For example, about one hundred old ships per year are broken and scrapped in Turkey's shipyards (Bailey 2000). China, India, Bangladesh, and Pakistan are Turkey's main competitors in attracting these shipbreaking jobs. Old ships contain hazardous materials, such as asbestos and toxic paints, and the process of breaking a ship is dangerous. Regulations in the industrial countries make shipbreaking extremely costly. Hence, shipping companies export their old vessels to developing countries, including Turkey, for breaking. Turkish authorities, presumably for economic reasons, have systematically failed to invoke a 1995 ban regarding the imports of hazardous waste to Turkey, as well as the Basel Convention on the Control of Transboundary Movements of Hazardous Waste (1989), which prohibits the export of such hazardous material.

A last example of how Western economic interests affect Turkish water resources is marine pollution caused by the heavy shipping traffic and consequent accidents in the Bosphorus Straits. According to th Turkish Maritime Pilots' Association, over 150 marine traffic accidents occurred between 1988–92 in the Bosphorus Straits (Turk

Kilavuz Kaptanlar Dernegi, 1999). In spite of several measures taken by the Turkish authorities, two accidents in 1994 and 1999 resulted in massive oil spills, fires, and marine pollution. Accidents and the routine release of contaminated water by ships in the Bosphorus Straits, the Marmara, and the Black Sea continue causing environmental damage with an estimated cleanup cost of $15 billion in 2000.

Soil and Land

Soil erosion and deforestation have been two major contributors to land degradation in Turkey. According to the Turkish National Environmental Action Plan, "About 73 percent of cultivated land and 68 percent of prime agricultural land are prone to erosion. Stream bank erosion affects 57.1 million hectares while wind erosion degrades another 466,000 hectares. As a result, about one billion tons of soil are carried away each year" (1999, 39).

Only 24 percent of Turkey's land surface is suitable for cultivation because of its limited soil depth. Erosion continually takes away a critical soil mass. As the liberalization policies neglect agriculture, and rural poverty rises, the clearing of land, overgrazing, and the use of wood as heating fuel will exacerbate the deterioration of soil and land quality. The intensified use of fertilizers and pesticides will only worsen this deterioration.

Forests cover only 26 percent of Turkey's surface area, and given the low and declining wood harvest ratio and the low level of roundwood production, reforestation promises to be a very slow process (National Environmental Action Plan 1998, 43). Deforestation has been further hastened by the increase in the production of wood-related products. Table 4.1 reflects the alarming increase in the production of wood and related products.

Deforestation also leads to watershed degradation, since forests help maintain water quality. Thanks to the Ataturk dam (the world's tenth largest), the Tigris and Euphrates watershed in the area lost 100 percent of its original forest cover (World Resources Institute 2001, 102).

Given the magnitude of the environmental degradation and the low quality of air, water, and land resources, it is naturally expected that Turkey's record regarding biodiversity would not be impressive. According to the World Resources Institute (2001, 244–50), 15 percent of the known mammal species, 5 percent of bird species, 18 percent of the reptiles, 28 percent of the known amphibians, 12 percent of the freshwater fish, and 25 percent of plants are threatened species. Turkey has very few protected areas, covering only .3 percent of the national territory. Continuing industrialization and urbanization, and agricultural practices associated with the increase in rural poverty, such as land clearing, poor irrigation practices, and overgrazing, all contribute in varying degrees to the declining biodiversity and ecological conditions in Turkey.

Thus, post-1980 policies have been a major factor in declining environmental quality, by increasing poverty, especially rural poverty, and by increasing economic growth without the necessary regulatory and supervisory institutions to limit environmental damage. This does not mean, however, that the Turkish public sector did not contribute to the environmental degradation. Having played such an important part in the Turkish industrialization process, it has been one of the primary contributors. Unfortunately lack of data does not allow for estimating the public sector's direct contribution to the worsening environmental conditions in Turkey.

Economic growth has especially contributed to the increase in energy consumption (Table 4.3). In the last decade, overall energy consumption rose by 54 percent. Oil accounted for 43.9 percent of this consumption, with coal at 26.7 percent and natural gas at 13.2 percent but rising. The production of energy, however, lagged behind and went up by only 11 percent, increasing Turkey's dependency on energy imports.

Western sources have continued to blame public sector involvement in the energy sector for the inefficiencies in Turkey's energy production and consumption. The US Energy Information Administration summarizes this view: "Because the Turkish energy sector is mainly state-owned, critics charge that the government's pricing policy has encouraged the inefficient use of energy" (2002, 2).

A close look at energy prices in selected OECD countries, however, does not support this argument. Available comparative data on energy prices for domestic and industrial use shows that Turkey has been pricing natural gas, heavy fuel oil, electricity and gasoline consistently higher than the OECD and non-OECD countries (OECD 1999a, 75). The only exception is coal used for heat and electricity generation. The price of Turkish coal is significantly lower than in other countries. The continuing encouragement of the use of coal is discouraging from an environmental point of view but understand-

Table 4.3. Energy Production and Consumption

Energy Production (1000 metric toe)					
From All Sources			From NonRenewable Energy Sources		
1987	1997	% change	Solid Fuels	Liquid Fuels	Gaseous Fuels
24,825	27,556	11%	13,118	3,525	208

Energy Consumption (1000 metric toe)					
From All Sources			From NonRenewable Energy Sources		
1987	1997	% change	Solid Fuels	Liquid Fuels	Gaseous Fuels
46,281	71,273	54%	21,176	30,863	8,339

Energy Consumption by Economic Sector (% of total consumption)					
	All Industries	Iron and Steel	Transportation	Agriculture	Commercial and Public Services	Residenti
1987	27.7	3.9	22.9	4.9	1.3	40.0
1997	33.7	3.8	22.8	5.3	2.8	31.4

Renewable Energy (1000 toe)					
Consumption			Production		
1987	1997	% change	1987	1997	% change
9,558	10,705	12%	9,309	10,705	15%

Source: World Resources Institute (2001).

able from a political perspective. In order to support growing industry and provide heating fuel for those who cannot afford the higher natural gas prices, subsidizing coal has been a critical political choice.

In 1997, Turkey's gasoline prices ranked fifteenth on a list of thirty-two countries, according to the International Energy Agency (1999). But by 1999, the US dollar price of a liter of regular gasoline at the pump had reached $1, the average European Union price (Mesutoglu 2001, 6). In addition, the share of various taxes in the price per liter gasoline in 1999 was 72 percent, close to the European Union average and significantly higher than in the United States.

These comparisons do not result from inefficiencies in the production, pricing, and distribution of energy in Turkey, but from deliberate pricing policy. For instance, Turkish authorities, bowing to the automotive industry lobby, have kept the price of unleaded gasoline higher than leaded gasoline, thereby encouraging the use of leaded. Only after mid–1993 did unleaded gasoline prices fall below leaded gasoline (Mesutoglu 2001, 22–24). It is hoped that the automotive industry and the authorities will phase out the use of leaded gasoline entirely in the near future.

Excess demand for energy has been chronic since the 1980s but has been decreasing since the late 1990s. An increase in electricity generation using renewable energy sources has helped close the energy gap. In spite of the environmental, cultural, and political problems of using dams to create hydroelectricity, projects like GAP (Southeast Anatolian Project) have helped increase electricity production. In addition, a 1997 law has allowed build-own-operate and build-own-transfer schemes to attract private, domestic, and foreign interests in the energy sector.

The environmental conditions in Turkey described here definitely do not inspire optimism. Years of collective negligence, at home and abroad, have taken their toll on the quality of available natural resources. Restoring and then maintaining sustainability calls for a concerted effort from all parties involved, domestic and foreign.

INDUSTRIALIZATION AND TRADE

Economic growth, accompanied by high and rapid industrial development, inevitably affects the physical environment. Hence, it is important to assess the environmental impact of economic policies in general and of economic liberalization and industrialization policies in particular. Unfortunately the lack of sufficiently systematic and consistently compiled longitudinal data on environmental variables and on industrial production at the 4–digit SITC level (Standard Industrial Trade Classification, referring to the detail in the composition of commodity classification groups) renders this assessment difficult. Until 1996, the United Nations Statistical Division published production statistics at the 4–digit SITC level, but then replaced it with a 6–digit classification, breaking data continuity. As it stands now, the State Institute of Statistics in Turkey publishes production data at the 3–digit level and export data at the 2–digit level, while UN production statistics remain at the 6–digit level. Lack of consistency among different data sources makes the investigation of the relationship between production of industrial goods and environmental degradation, as well as the relationship between trade in industrial goods and environmental degradation, a monumental task. Still, we can intuit that the industries that grew rapidly in the post-1980 period have been the relatively dirty and high pollutant ones. Furthermore, we can hypothesize that trade has provided the modus operandi behind this increase in industrial production. Industrial countries, especially in the European Union, more concerned with human health and the quality of life in their own countries and having stricter environmental regulations, have increased the imports of "dirty" goods from developing countries in the last two decades or so. To some extent, the Summers blunder described above reflects reality. The migration of "dirty" industries is a fact, and Summers's economic explanation, in the neoclassical mold, is that people discount the value of life in developing countries and so are less concerned with the long-run effects of pollution there.

In the early 1990s, Lucas, Wheeler and Hettige (1992) and Wheeler and Martin (1993) listed pollution intensity estimates for 4–digit manufacturing industries in the United States. The studies focused on three pollution intensity indicators: biological oxygen demand (BOD), total suspended particulate (TSP), and toxic pollutants (TOX), using them to investigate how industrial production in the United States affected the environment. BOD measures damage to aquatic life, TSP the degradation of air quality, and TOX total toxic emissions. Odekon (1996) applied their study to Turkish manufacturing industries. Assuming that the production technology is similar, since Turkey imports it from industrial countries, this 1996 study looked at whether the fastest-growing manufacturing industries from 1980–92 were relatively green or dirty, based on these three intensity indicators. The study found that the three dirty industries, iron and steel, nonferrous metals, and metal products, ranked among the top ten high-growth industries (with an overall average growth rate of 11.5 percent). Industry growth rates and pollution intensities significantly correlate in Turkey. High growth industries also have high TSP and TOX intensities, especially damaging air and land quality. The corresponding Spearman Rank correlation coefficients are .07 and .06, respectively. Both coefficients are significant at .05 percent. The study also showed that the dirty industries were at the same time high-growth export industries and concluded was that dirty industries from European industrial countries have migrated to Turkey.

We extend that study here, using the available Turkish State Institute of Statistics data in order to draw on a consistent data set for the

1991–98 period. An immediately evident change in the 1990s, relative to the previous decade, is the significant decrease in the growth of manufacturing activity. The economic slowdown in Turkey and Europe in the 1990s lowered the annual average manufacturing industry growth rate to around 4.0 percent, down from approximately 9.0 percent. Nevertheless, the three dirty industries' growth rates remained above the industry average. During 1991–98, iron and steel grew by 5.0, nonferrous metals by 5.2, and metal products by 7.1 percent. The economic slowdown has not prevented the Turkish manufacturing industry from accelerating production of relatively dirty goods.

As already mentioned, export orientation has been a defining characteristic of post-1980 economic liberalization policy in Turkey. Several key aspects of export orientation are captured in Figures 4.2–4.4. The traditional pre-1980 emphasis on agricultural exports has shifted to manufacturing exports, which sharply increased until 1987 and thereafter stabilized (Figure 4.2). Europe has been the primary export market for Turkey. In the early 1980s, the Iran-Iraq war stimulated Turkish exports to that area but only until 1986. The share of exports to North America increased, as it did to former Soviet Russia (Figure 4.3). Textiles have traditionally been the primary export commodities, but basic metal, manufactured metals, and chemicals

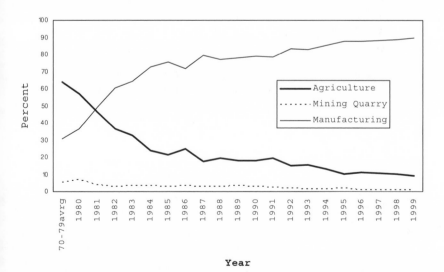

Figure 4.2. Export Composition
Source: UN, *International Trade Statistics,* various issues.

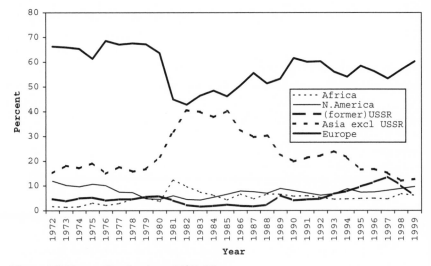

Figure 4.3. Export Destinations, 1972–99
Source: *International Trade Statistics,* various issues.

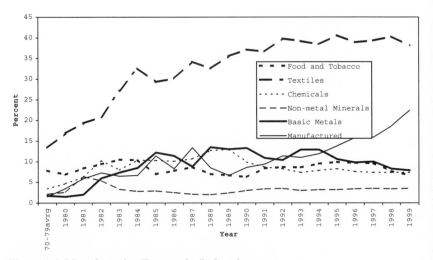

Figure 4.4. Manufacturing Exports by Industries
Source: *International Trade Statistics,* various issues.

have gained prominence, as have other manufacturing exports during the postliberalization era (Figure 4.4).

The relationship between the environment and trade is, at the very least, a controversial one, and several studies have focused on the environmental impact of trade (for surveys see J. Dean 1992; UNEP [UN Environmental Program] 2000; IISP [International Institute of Sustainable Development] 2000; Cole 2000). Environmentalists maintain that free trade contributes to environmental deterioration for several reasons. First, international trade increases production and consumption and hence raises resource use in ways not environmentally friendly. Second, as trade intensifies so does transportation, and creating more pollution. Third, as the pollution haven hypothesis argues (and as we do in this chapter), trade between countries with differing regulatory frameworks causes pollution-intensive industries to concentrate in countries with less stringent regulations. This concentration can involve the actual migration of dirty industries to developing countries and/or increased imports of dirty industry goods from developing countries.

The proponents of free trade, on the other hand, argue that the welfare-maximizing effects of free trade would create enough additional resources for pollution abatement and for the adoption of green technology in developing countries (see Dasgupta and Maler 1995). This group also maintains that the adverse environmental effects of free trade result from trade-distorting policies pursued in developing countries. Free market–oriented economic policies would eliminate these self-inflicted, unwanted effects of trade on the environment.

The few empirical studies regarding the subject fail to bring any clarity to the environment-trade dilemma. Birdsall and Wheeler (1993), for example, found that pollution intensity growth was relatively low in fast-growing open economies in the 1980s. Lucas, Wheeler and Hettige (1992, 88) concluded that "the effect of trade policies is pollution decreasing for some and pollution increasing for others and on average would be pollution neutral." Ferrantino and Linkins (1999) showed that liberalization reduces global pollution moderately but relocates dirty production to developing countries. Xu and Song (2000), on the other hand, could not find any clear evidence to support the pollution haven hypothesis. Finally, Low and Yeats (1992) concluded that the share of the dirty industries in developing country exports has increased in the 1980s.

In Turkey, the early 1980s marked an unprecedented rise in the exports of goods from the three dirty industries. From 1980–87, 27 percent of manufacturing exports originated from the dirty iron and steel, nonferrous metals, and metal products industries. The average growth rate of exports from these industries reached a record 70 percent (Table 4.4). This strong export performance attracted the OECD's attention. In a study on expanding and declining manufacturing sectors in Turkey, the OECD concluded, "Turkey experienced particularly strong output growth in sectors such as iron and steel, basic metals and fabricated metal products that have been performing relatively poorly in the OECD area" (1994, 85). Thus, in a roundabout way the OECD admitted to the migration of dirty European industries to Turkey.

In the 1990s, the economic slowdown in the OECD countries, and to some extent the tightening of environmental regulations in Turkey, have contributed to a significant drop in the export growth rates of dirty industries, to an average of 14.4 percent. These factors also reduced the share of dirty industries in total manufacturing exports to 14.4 percent (Table 4.4). Even though the growth rate is significantly lower than the 70 percent of the 1980s, it still indicates a very strong pace. Environmental degradation has slowed but is still continuing.

Industrial OECD countries have successfully exported some of their pollution to Turkey by increasing their imports from Turkish dirty industries. Authorities need to assess the environmental damage and shift the abatement costs proportionally to industrial OECD countries. Developing countries subjected to the migration of dirty industries might even think of cooperating to bring a case to the World Trade Organization and other relevant international forums, like the UN and the human rights courts, since all individuals, irrespective of the level of industrialization in their home country, have

Table 4.4. Export Performance of "Dirty" Industries: Growth of Exports and Share in Manufacturing Exports, 1980–87 and 1991–98 (average annual percent)

	Growth Rate of Exports		Share in Manufacturing Exports	
	1980–87	1991–98	1980–87	1991–98
Iron and Steel	96.6	6.3	19.4	11.1
Nonferrous Metals	35.3	14.2	3.3	1.4
Metal Manufactures	78.3	22.7	4.3	1.9

Source: SIS, various issues.

a natural right to a clean environment. Industrial countries need to be held accountable for the damage they have caused to the environment and to human health in developing countries.

POLICY MEASURES

Environmental problems in Turkey are abundant. Authorities have become aware of the need to contain the environmental damage inflicted by years of neglect. Examples of appropriate policy actions already taken include the 1983 Environmental Law, which is based on the "polluter pays" principle; the formation of the Ministry of the Environment in 1991; laws enacted to protect environmentally sensitive areas and control hazardous waste; laws governing water products and national parks and forests; conservation laws; and numerous regulations controlling water pollution and air quality (Yeldan and Balkan 1993; OECD Economic Survey 2000). Turkey has been a signatory to several international treaties (but not the Kyoto Protocol) and has adopted a National Environmental Action Plan (1999). These are steps in the right direction. However, all these rules and regulations necessitate an efficient and effective institutional framework and a well-trained cadre of civil servants. Unless these requirements are met, the "polluter pays" principle could easily be corrupted into a bribery-driven "payer-pollutes" scheme.

Poverty, lack of public awareness, lack of transparency and accountability, industrialization policies, coal subsidies, and migration of foreign dirty industries all contribute to environmental degradation. Eliminating poverty should probably be the first line of attack to limit environmental damage, but the post-1980 liberalization and industrialization policies have increased poverty and hurt the environment. It is imperative that Turkey reviews its economic policies and starts emphasizing distributive efficiency, rather than be carried away by an emphasis on allocative efficiency as dictated by the IMF and the World Bank.

Environmental education must start in the classroom at the elementary level teaching the younger generation the importance of environmental sustainability. School curricula at every level should formally include an environmental education component. The UN Development Program (UNDP) has been promoting the organization of environmental nongovernmental organizations (NGOs) in Turkey for the purpose of educating the public. As long as the NGOs are independently financed and are willing to oppose the interests of the domestic and international business elites when needed, they may indeed help disseminate useful environmental information in an effective way and help educate the public.

Turkey is already making use of alternative energy resources as mentioned before. Further investment in geothermal and hydro energy would pay dividends in the future. The expansion in these renewable energy sources should be in the core of the national energy policy. The build-own-operate and build-own-transfer schemes that international financial organizations and institutions promoted in Turkey in the last decade are examples of their tendency to promote fossil fuel–based energy systems that would benefit the energy producers in the industrial countries. As Vallette and Wysham (2002) show, the World Bank has financed several energy projects in the last decade that promoted coal, oil, and gas-based power plants. Only a minuscule portion of the projects financed by the Bank involved alternative, renewable energy sources. It would be an uphill battle but Turkish authorities should insist on an independent national green-energy policy and should seek financing to expand the alternative energy source base of the country. This approach would reduce the dependency on foreign energy and would also promote domestic employment in the relatively labor-intensive alternative energy industry.

Migration of dirty industries is an international problem and needs to be addressed at the international level by industrial and developing countries alike in such a way that the environmental standards in both groups of countries would be similar but would also allow for differences in the local conditions. Neoclassical economic principles and policies focusing on allocative efficiency fail to recognize the unfairness inherent in the migration of dirty industries. These industries are a perfect example of negative externalities at the international level, and Turkey and other developing countries should be compensated for the damages they have had to endure.

We have given other evidence for how industrial countries have contributed to worsening environmental quality in Turkey: Eurogold, the Bosphorus Straits, Italian toxic barrels, and shipbreaking. Western influence on environmental quality in developing countries needs to be regulated at an international level. This would be achieved only if decision making at international organizations, such as the IMF, World Bank, and WTO, is democratized, so developing countries gain equal rights with the industrial countries at the policy level.

Moreover, if Turkey seriously envisions joining the European Union, it must be prepared to adopt the EU laws on environment. The EU laws and regulations on chemicals and waste, air and water quality, acidification, natural resources, unleaded gasoline, climate change, and biodiversity are numerous and very strict. They contain relatively costly mandates that Turkey will eventually need to adopt. Given the EU stance regarding the Kyoto Protocol, Turkey will have to sign it too. During the phase-in period, it will have to prepare itself for specific greenhouse policies, including emission standards, abatement strategy, and emission trading schemes. These are costly but needed initiatives that await Turkey.

The IMF recommendations regarding privatization implicitly address environmental issues as well—implicitly, because none of the letters of intent has any explicit reference to any environmental problem or concern. The IMF, the bastion of allocative efficiency, assumes that most environmental ills result from inefficiencies in production, especially by state economic enterprises. A private-property owner would equate marginal benefit of a resource to its marginal cost and thus optimize the allocative efficiency. It would not benefit the private owner of a resource to overuse it. Hence, privatization would eliminate excessive environmental degradation. What this approach fails to recognize, however, is that because of the externalities, it is almost impossible to calculate the marginal benefits and costs of natural resource use in dollar terms. Privatization for the sake of allocative efficiency becomes an excuse to transfer wealth to the economic elite.

In Turkey, coal, petroleum, electricity, and other sources of energy are either completely or partly owned by the state, and the IMF has targeted these enterprises for privatization. For reasons we already mentioned, it is true that coal use, especially that of lignite coal, has been artificially promoted by below-market-pricing policies by a state-owned economic enterprise. This does not mean, however, that the entire energy sector in the economy should be privatized. For instance, the privatization of the iron and steel industry may or may not affect the environment. If privatization means that new green technology will immediately be installed, then pollution intensity in the industry may decrease. Otherwise, reaching allocative efficiency with the old and dirty technology would not make a significant dent in the pollution intensity of an industry. A state-run enterprise could attain efficiency, and indeed Turkish public companies have significantly improved their efficiency record.

The political economy of privatization and of a market economy does not necessarily lead to either equitable allocation of essential resources or environmental safeguards of those resources. The reigning principle in a market economy is that those who can afford it have the right to consume. Elsewhere, privatization in the energy sector and of other utilities has eliminated the poor from the market. Two big French multinationals, Suez Lyonnaise des Eaux and Vivendi-Generale des Eaux have taken control of utilities, especially water, in several developing countries in Latin America, Africa, and Asia. They have taken advantage of the WTO's Qatar agreement of November 2001, Article 31 of which articulated the need for the reduction or elimination of tariff and nontariff barriers to environmental goods and services (Le Monde Diplomatique 2002, 13). As a result, in countries penetrated by these two multinationals, the poor have lost whatever access they had to water and to other utilities because of significant rate hikes by the two French companies. Lack of heat, electricity, and water aggravates health and sanitation conditions for the poor and thus worsens the environment. The point is that in a developing country, limited income and the right to basic needs do call for the public provision of fundamental necessities.

Development literature perceives environmental degradation more as the result of actions by the poverty-stricken groups. It stresses the practices and socioeconomic characteristics of the rural and urban poor, such as low education and high population growth rate, and formulates policies targeting them. Turkey is a mid-income developing country and has a sizable and mature industrial sector. The industrial sector must now be held responsible for its contribution to environmental degradation and made to pay for the damages it has inflicted.

The National Environment Action Plan of Turkey (1999) is an ambitious document that diagnoses the environmental problems and prioritizes environmental policies. It attests to the fact that Turkish authorities, at least on paper, have a full understanding of the need for sustainability of Turkey's natural capital and of the measures needed to achieve it. If domestic and international financial resources can be energized to meet the projected $300 million initial cost, Turkey would be taking a giant step toward sustainability.

5

Why Liberalization?

I n the previous four chapters, we showed that economic liberalization in Turkey has been far from successful. Inflation and unemployment remain relatively high. The attempt to improve the balance of payments has been limited. Foreign direct investment is not
only low but exists primarily in the form of speculative portfolio investment. The agricultural sector has transformed itself as dictated by
Western industrial countries. Industrialization has meant growth in
dirty industries—again, a pattern imposed by Western industrial
countries. One inevitably wonders why the IMF and World Bank continue pushing for economic liberalization, and why Turkey and other
developing countries continue to act as submissively as they have for
the past two decades.

The search for answers to these questions starts with an analysis of
the world economic system within which developing countries operate. It also requires an analysis of the political economy of liberalization in such countries. This chapter begins with a critical review of
various selected post–World War II approaches to economic development; then describes the political economy of liberalization in
Turkey; and focuses on the relations among economic liberalization,
political and economic democracy, and human rights;* and finally,
discusses potential institutional reforms that would incorporate labor
directly into the development process as an economic and social partner with global capital.

Perspectives on Economic Development

In the post–World War II period, economic development was approached from various broad perspectives. Here, we look at four

*I thank the Honorable Riza Turmen, judge on the European Court of Human
Rights, for his contribution to this chapter.

125

main theoretical schools: the traditionalist school, the dependency school, the world-systems school, and the neoliberal school.

The forefather of the traditionalist society–based approach was the American economic historian W. Rostow (1960), who argued that in non-Western societies, poverty, perpetuated by traditional economic, social, and political relationships, hinders economic development. According to his stage theory, escape from this cycle lies in a push toward a so-called "takeoff," where the economy reaches an investment-output ratio higher than 10 percent and enters a stage of self-sustained growth. Contemporaries of Rostow developed similar theories, arguing that modernization is the key to economic development. Max Weber (1958) saw religious tradition—specifically the lack of a "Protestant Ethic"—as preventing development in non-Western economies. Other dualistic development theories blamed the traditional sector for lacking necessary modern, urban characteristics, making them lag behind the modern sector (see Boeke 1953). This social inertia, the cause of "backwardness," could be overcome only with some form of "push." Push-based theories in development are abundant. Nurkse (1953), Hirschman (1958), and Leibenstein (1957), among others, have proposed forms of a "big push." In Leibenstein's critical minimum-effort hypothesis, foreign investment and new technology would provide the big push, while Nurkse and Hirschman's balanced vs. unbalanced growth hypothesis emphasized the importance of leading key sectors in the development process. These leading sectors would provide the source from which growth spreads through the economy. Interestingly, push-based theories have repeatedly and explicitly called for a strong state role in the development process.

The implicit assumption in these arguments is that modernity, as defined by the development experience of Western industrial countries, is the essential prerequisite for development. One of the major characteristics of this conception of modern society is an openness to change that in effect institutionalizes the change. This "modern" orientation provides the social, cultural, political, and economic environment and the necessary set of values and institutions to promote industrialization, growth, and development. This Western-centered view of economic development is reflected in most post–World War II growth models. Drawing on the experience of Western industrial countries, growth models emphasize the importance of capital accumulation, savings, reinvestment, and technology in achieving the desired growth in income. Classic examples are the Harrod-Domar and

Solow growth models (see Taylor 1979). They, like all classical and neoclassical models, focus solely on income growth and on efficiency in production and consumption without an explicit concern for distributional issues, perceiving an economic system that pays factors of production according to their marginal productivities as a just and fair arrangement.

This was, in short, the state of mainstream development economics in the late 1970s, a concerted effort to blame the developing countries for lacking what it takes to develop the impetus for modernity. This Weltanschauung also contained an implicit message: the supremacy of the Western industrialized world over the developing non-Western world—a prejudice that would be exacerbated over time.

The dependency school, on the other hand, placed the core-periphery relationship at the center of development analysis. As early as 1950, Raul Prebish, the head of the United Nations Economic Commission for Latin America, argued that the pattern of trade between Latin American countries and the industrial world made the developing countries dependent on imports of consumer goods. This dependency resulted from the deterioration in the terms of trade against Latin American economies, which limited their industrialization efforts. Even though Prebish's arguments provided the foundation for import-substitution-industrialization, it was Andre Gunder Frank (1966) who brought the dependency paradigm to the attention of the English-speaking world (Bentley 1997). His metropolis-satellite model, the basis of the "development of underdevelopment" paradigm, reacted against the post–World War II mainstream view that the underdeveloped world remained underdeveloped because of its own internal characteristics. Frank put it eloquently: "The modernization school assumes that there is something wrong inside Third World countries—such as traditional culture, overpopulation, little investment, and lack of achievement motivation—and this is why Third World countries are backward and stagnant" (1966, 96).

According to Frank, this myopic view of world history ignores how the developing countries' colonial experiences determined their economic destiny in the development process. In Frank's model, the accumulation of capital in the industrialized core leads it to continuously seek cheaper resources and raw materials in the periphery. With the partnership of the local elite, the periphery's economic surplus is systematically extracted from the periphery to the core, retarding industrialization and development in the periphery and only benefiting the core and the periphery's elite. This role of the local elite reinforces the social and economic relations of production, appropriation, and distribution of economic surplus perpetuating a well-defined distribution of labor and class structure that only benefits capital. This relationship dates from colonial days but continues into modern times. In a sense, development in the Western world depends on underdevelopment in the developing world inasmuch as it siphons off the surplus value. In this process the capitalists in the periphery play the role of intermediary, acting on behalf of the international metropolis. In each periphery, national metropolises with their own peripheries form an efficient network that serves the international metropolis rather than the periphery.

Within this framework, underdevelopment becomes imposed by both external conditions (the unequal relationship between the core and peripheral countries) and internal conditions (the domestic sociopolitical and economic dynamics; Dos Santos 1970; Amin 1976; Petras 1979). Consequently, the policy recommendation of the dependency paradigm is for peripheral countries to sever ties with the industrial core in order to accumulate the necessary domestic capital for industrialization.

Wallerstein (1975 and 1979) transferred the periphery-core model from the realm of colonial relationships to the framework of a capitalist world-economy, where modern industrial countries constitute the capitalist core and developing countries belong to either the semiperiphery or periphery, depending on their social, political, and economic development. By expanding the core-periphery model to world systems, his model helps explain the exchange relations between the capitalist core and noncolonized semiperipheral or peripheral countries like Turkey, as well as post-1980 globalization and its dynamics. While Wallerstein originally proposed that the capitalist core is an amalgam of all the industrial capitalist countries, this view is now being challenged. Chase-Dunn (1996), for instance, distinguishes between the core-wide empire and the hegemonic core state, with economic-political-military power concentrated in the hands of a single superpower. In the contemporary world, the question is whether the core is a homogeneous and peaceful coalition of the United States and European industrial countries, or whether the core itself is undergoing a period of friction, with the United States trying to assert its hegemonic power over the other industrial countries. Some argue that globalization is a direct extension of the United States' ambition to form a hegemonic empire to control international financial and economic relations and outcomes, thereby maintaining high profitability for American and global financial and capital markets, as well as for transnational corporations (TNCs; Gowan 1999). According to Gowan, the United States has formed an unequal partnership with the European Union in the capitalist core, with the United States playing CEO and defining the relationships among core countries, as well as those between the core and the semi-periphery and periphery. Within this framework, Gowan regards Japan as a third party in the core that the United States considers a potential rival and therefore keeps under control. China, though emerging as a potential core rival, does not enter Gowan's analysis.

Hardt and Negri, on the other hand, oppose the view of a competitive core and emphasize its homogeneity: "We think it is important to note that what used to be conflict and competition among several imperialist powers has in important respects been replaced by the idea of a single power that overdetermines them all, structures them in a unitary way, and treats them under one common notion of right that is decidedly postcolonial and postimperialist" (2000, 19).

A separate issue concerning the core-periphery-based dependency paradigm is whether it would lead to convergence or divergence between the core and the periphery. Fukuyama (1991) and Huntington (1996) have written extensively on this issue. If the core's supremacy is unconditionally accepted by the periphery (convergence), we may witness the "end of history" suggested by Fukuyama. If not, the resulting divergence may bring Huntington's "clash of civilizations."

Figure 5.1 shows the current organization of the core-periphery relationship, including the contemporary debate on neoliberalism and the US global hegemony. In the core are the United States, the European Union, and Japan. The United States, however, has separated itself from the EU and Japan by establishing a hegemonic position, thanks to its economic and military power. It could be argued that within the United States, the Treasury Department, the Federal Reserve, and Wall Street design the economic strategy and the Pentagon designs the military strategy. Informal but powerful consortiums such as the World Economic Forum, and the G-5, G-7, G-8, and G-11 summits of the finance ministers and the heads of the industrial states, set the political, economic, and social agenda, and policy principles at the global level that facilitate the free mobility of international financial capital. The IMF, the World Bank, WTO, OECD, NAFTA, and the EU act on behalf of international financial capital, implementing the core's policies in the semiperiphery and periphery countries with the cooperation of the periphery's restructured na-

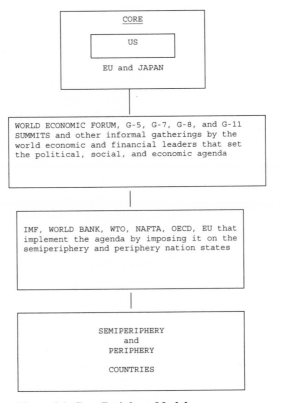

Figure 5.1. Core-Periphery Model

tion states and their economic, political, and military elite, which have formed common interests with the elite in the core. Consequently, surplus is systematically transferred from the periphery and semiperiphery to the international metropolises in the core.

Interestingly, in spite of their once taboo neo-Marxist overtones, the dependency and world system paradigms had a wide audience among intellectuals as well as the political and business elite. After all, import-substitution-industrialization arose from these discussions. The Korean War, the Vietnam War, oil shocks, high inflation and unemployment, political instability, and Watergate provided a crisis environment in the sixties and seventies that tolerated economic soul-searching and exploring alternatives.

The neoliberal counterrevolution of the 1980s emerged as a reaction to this tolerant environment of the 1960s and 1970s. It emphasized free markets and the minimization of government's role in the economy. As mentioned before, the Washington Consensus provided the blueprint, and the World Bank and the IMF the institutional means, to spread neoliberal development strategy in the developing world. Neoliberalism could also be seen as a response to the 1970s economic slowdown in the core industrial countries. Post–World War II expansion came to an abrupt halt with the two oil price increases in the 1970s. Corporate profitability decreased significantly, prompting the start of globalization in the early 1980s, which aimed to restore profitability, through free movement of capital at a global level. To this end, globalization targeted labor in core, semiperipheral, and peripheral countries. Lower wages, benefits, and job security, and diminished unionization and labor rights, all contributed to the so-called "labor market flexibility" that helped reduce labor costs and recover corporate profitability.

By minimizing the traditional role of the government, the neoliberal paradigm has opened developing economies to the whims of transnational corporations and reinforced current trends in trade and privatization. For the same reason, it also has led to the reemergence of unequal exchange and exploitation discourses among the progressive, leftist intelligentsia (see Gowan 1999; Hardt and Negri 2000; Petras 2000), who analyze globalization in terms of a class struggle between labor and capital and emphasize the exploitation of labor by capital at a global level. The concepts of class struggle and exploitation have found a new home in the "neo-imperial" discussions, which regard neo-imperialism as the modus operandi behind exploitation-cum-globalization. An additional unique characteristic of the neoliberal paradigm has been the extent of its implementation. Under the auspices of the IMF and the World Bank, and under the rubric of economic liberalization, it has penetrated almost the entire spectrum of developing countries, from China to Turkey.

At a different level, however, all four of these schools of development we discussed have a common denominator: they all focus on capital and wealth accumulation. The traditionalist school, which emphasizes the importance of modernization, calls for developing countries to change their value system so as to facilitate capital accumulation and the transition to the capitalist development phase. This process would in fact be helped by the industrial countries, which would take their share in the process. The dependency and world systems hypotheses, on the other hand, claim that the industrial world hinders the entire development process because of its own need to accumulate capital. Relatively cheap natural resources and/or labor that the developing countries provide raise the profits of the industrialized countries, which would otherwise have stagnated at home because of increasing production costs, postponing the collapse of the capitalist system. The neoliberal paradigm focuses on unifying markets at the global level to allow international capital full freedom and mobility to facilitate the transfer of profits (surplus) from the periphery and the semiperiphery to the core.

THE POLITICAL ECONOMY OF LIBERALIZATION

The neoliberal agenda to internationalize production and movements of capital led to privatization, curbing of labor rights, reduction of real wages, and an increased role for international development organizations, such as the IMF, World Bank, and WTO. As time went on, the ensuing concentration of wealth and capital within both developing and industrial countries reached unprecedented levels. This concentration increased the need for expansion of surplus value, leading to further liberalization and globalization. The idea was to secure access to financial markets once and for all, anywhere and anytime. Having learned from its past mistakes, neoliberalism targeted one by one the institutions and groups that questioned it in the 1960s and 1970s. Through the IMF and the World Bank, state institutions were restructured to support the neoliberal agenda. International agreements in trade and other spheres created a new order whereby the nation state became directly supportive of the world system and the TNCs. As a result, economies in the peripheral and semiperipheral countries have undergone massive structural changes; for example, a new entrepreneurial class specializing in international finance and trade emerged as an important part of the "national bourgeoisie" in all developing countries (Albo 2002; Grabel 2002; Petras 2000; Petras and Veltmeyer 2001; Foster 2002). Economic liberalization and internationalization of production and financial markets constitute the heart of the neoliberal ideology. However, concentration of wealth and capital accumulation has led universally to increasing economic inequality. Petras and Veltmeyer summarized the distributive aspect of neoliberal ideology: "The world ascendancy of globalist classes has provoked a serious social crisis affecting wage workers, peasants, employees and self-employed throughout the world. The growth and penetration of globalist policies have engendered a significant increase in inequality between the minority within the globalist loop and those exploited by it" (2001, 50).

Within this contemporary world economic system, Turkey finds itself a semiperipheral country. Actually, we could argue, using Wallerstein's terminology (1975, 80), that Turkey has gained semiperipheral status by invitation, since in 1980 Prime Minister Özal returned to Turkey from the IMF with the mandate to initiate the liberalization program. Similarly, Dervis subsequently came from the World Bank to further the liberalization program. The economic attractiveness of Turkey for the core stems from its being a middle-income, semi-industrialized country with cheaper labor than in Europe and the United States, and a large and young lucrative export market. Turkey is a suitable financial center for facilitating the turnover of the core's financial capital. As we have seen in the previous chapters, it has been a successful semiperipheral country, serving the core well and earning rewards for this service. These rewards, however, have not been distributed equitably. Hence, the question we turn to next is who has become better off and who has suffered as a result of post-1980 policies in Turkey.

We have already shown the deterioration in Turkey's income distribution. Another indicator of economic inequality is the distribution of consumption expenditures by quintiles of population. In Turkey, according to the World Bank (2000, 283), the share of the lowest 40 percent of population in total consumption is 8.1 percent, whereas that of the top 20 percent is 47.7 percent, with the top 10 percent's share reaching 32.3 percent. The distribution of consumption expenditures by type is given in Table 5.1. The share of necessities (food, clothing, and housing) in total consumption expenditures is 87 percent for the lowest quintile but only 54 percent for the top quintile. Consumption expenditures on amenities rise as one moves to higher quintiles. However, the low level of public expenditure on health and education (2.2 percent of the GDP on education and 2.9 percent on health, compared with 4.4 percent on the military in 1998) indicates the low government concern with social welfare. Indeed, the percentages spent on education and health have not changed significantly over the past twenty years, despite the growth in population that has lowered the population's age.

The household survey data also reveal the types of income households receive. In 1994, labor income constituted 24 percent of total household earnings. The remaining non-labor income was classified as total entrepreneurial income in one category, and rent, interest,

Table 5.1. Distribution of Consumption Expenditures by Quintiles

	1994 (percent)				
	Lowest 20%	Second 20%	Third 20%	Fourth 20%	Top 20%
Food, beverage, tobacco	57	53	47	41	23
Clothing and footwear	4	7	9	10	10
Housing and rent	26	24	24	25	21
House furnishing	3	4	4	6	14
Health	2	2	2	3	3
Transportation	3	3	4	6	14
Entertainment and culture	0.4	1	1	2	4
Education	0.2	1	1	1	2
Hotel, restaurant	2	2	3	3	3
Other goods/services	2	4	5	5	7

Source: Calculated from SIS (1999, 671).

and transfers in another. In 1987, labor income's share was 24.07 percent, with rent, interest, and transfers adding up to 24.5 percent. This latter figure rose to 29.3 percent in 1994, as the concentration of wealth and income grew significantly. In addition, changes in the tax structure enabled the wealthier to pay less tax. The shares of wealth, inheritance, and assets tax in central government tax revenues dropped from 1992 to 1997, wealth tax revenues from 0.9 percent to 0.7 percent, assets tax from 85 percent to 3 percent, and inheritance tax from 19 to 8 percent. The asset tax revenue plunge to some extent results from of the 1994 economic crisis, but nevertheless, the drop in all three tax revenues indicates that the wealthy have been paying less. Furthermore, although the tax on earnings of individuals and corporations made up 40 percent of the total tax revenues in 1992–97, 80 percent of that was individual income tax (SIS, 1999). These tax figures indicate that Turkish corporations have successfully avoided the increases in their tax share proportionate to their share in the economy. This phenomenon constitutes another universal characteristic of economic liberalization (Petras and Veltmeyer 2001).

In a short period of time, from 1991 to 1998, the share of the financial sector in the economy rose sharply, from 2 percent of the GNP to 5 percent. Turkish banks and foreign joint ventures, Turkish insurance companies, stockbrokers, and factoring and leasing companies have enjoyed a deregulated financial environment since 1986. Conglomerate holdings, already established in banking via multiple bank ownerships, entered with ease into the non-bank financial markets. The growth in the financial sector also brought new opportunities to the national bourgeoisie. For instance, Sabanci and Koc, the usual Turkish names on *Forbes* magazine's list of the world's richest people were outranked in 2002 by Mehmet Karamehmet, a forty-eight-year-old finance and telecom tycoon (*Forbes* 2002).

Ten out of the twenty major industrial enterprises in Turkey are big public ventures, such as petroleum, coal, electricity, sugar, tobacco, and steel (Table 5.2). The other half comprises private enterprises in automotive, electronics, electrical appliances, and plastic products. The majority of the latter group has direct foreign partnerships, as reflected by their foreign names, while the rest have loyalty arrangements in place. The presence of foreign interests in itself, one could argue, is not a big problem. However, in a fully operative world system, Turkey's wealth and economic surplus are systematically transferred abroad along with profits. According to Somel (2003), roughly one-tenth of the economic surplus in Turkey is transferred abroad annually. Naturally, the major state economic enterprises, with their potential profit opportunities, attract the attention of the domestic and foreign business elite and more and more become targets for privatization.

While the rich get richer in this liberalization and globalization process, the economic disadvantages faced by labor and other low-income groups are deepening, predominantly because of the weakening of the nation-state and its replacement by the market-state. Rapidly diminishing public services and social welfare, the dismantling of the nuclear family, and shrinking economic opportunities conspire to marginalize labor and other economically disadvantaged groups such as the elderly. Layoffs and attrition add to unemployment, already on the rise as a result of anti-inflationary policies. The high unemployment rate, over 16 percent if disguised unemployment is included, becomes more of a problem in view of severe long-term unemployment, which has reached 46.1 percent of total female and 37.5 of male unemployment (World Bank 2000, 241). The deteriorating economic conditions have inevitably contributed to poverty. In 1994, the percent of the population earning below $1 a day was 2.4 percent, and below $2 a day 5 percent, the highest rate in the OECD (World Bank 2001).

**Table 5.2. Turkey's 20 Major Industrial Enterprises, 2000
(ranked in descending order)**

Enterprise	Industry
1. Tupras	petroleum refinery
2. TEAS	electricity
3. Oyak-Renault*	automotive
4. Arcelik*	consumer durables
5. Eregli Demir ve Celik	iron and steel
6. Tekel	tobacco and alcohol
7. Türkiye Seker Fabrikalari	sugar
8. Tofas Turk Otomobil Fabrikasi*	automotive
9. Petkim	petrochemicals
10. Vestel Elektronik*	electronics
11. Ford Otomativ Sanayi*	automotive
12. Turkiye Komur Isletmeleri	coal
13. Mercedes-Benz Turk Anonim St.*	automotive
14. Aygaz*	butane, durables
15. Turkiye Petrolleri Anonim Ort	petroleum
16. Beko Elektronik*	electronics
17. Iskenderun Demir ve Celik	iron and steel
18. SASA Dupont Sabanci Polyester Jan*	polyester
19. BSF Profilo Elektrikli Gerecler*	electrical appliances
20. Philsa Philip Morris Sabanci Sigara San*	tobacco

Source: Istanbul Chamber of Industry
* Indicates a private enterprise.

The economic decline of the economically disadvantaged groups clearly coincides with liberalization, privatization, and the restructuring of the nation-state. Though one could argue that economic efficiency requires these changes, the costs of such changes are borne asymmetrically, not by the groups that profit but by those that suffer. The fact that gains in allocative efficiency are paid for by the most vulnerable groups causes further distributional misallocation. Even though the Turkish public sector has not been economically efficient, a rational public sector can act as a catalyst to balance allocative and distributional efficiency and minimize the distributional costs of economic liberalization. The Turkish public sector, with a long history in the Turkish economy and Turkish society, could effectively and efficiently be enlisted to establish that balance.

An additional consequence of economic discontent, globalization, high urbanization, and Westernization in Turkey has been the rise of Islam as an economic, social, and political power. The religious groups that lost their visibility and importance in the post–1923 secular republic have started reemerging as a viable force in Turkish society, represented by an average of 12 to 14 percent of the popular vote in all post–1980 elections. The continuing popularity of religious political groups among the poor, in spite of the army's undemocratic attempts to suppress and dismantle their political infrastructure, is alarming, on the one hand because of the threat these religious groups pose to the secular republic, and on the other because of the disrespect "secular" and "Kemalist" groups display toward democratic principles.

The attractiveness of Islam to economically vulnerable groups derives from the teachings of Koran. Economic and social justice are important and observable elements within Islam's broader concept of "human justice." Sharp departures from religious injunctions or justice, such as a widening of the gap between the rich and the poor, provide an opportunity for religion to strengthen and spread. Social and economic injustices have not only strengthened the reemergent religious movements in Turkey but will continue to aggravate the country's social and economic problems unless the existing problems of poverty, inequality, and unfulfilled expectations are solved.

Nevertheless, a typical reaction to criticisms regarding liberalization's adverse distributional aspects is that liberalization has improved the overall quality of life. Every year the United Nations Development Program (UNDP) produces a volume on "human development" and ranks countries according to a taxonomic "human development index" (HDI). This weighted composite index incorporates various aspects of life, including life expectancy, education, and income. Unfortunately, it suffers from numerous technical measurement deficiencies common to all composite index calculations, and moreover, does not include measures of economic and social despair, or the exploitation of disadvantaged groups. The UNDP has in fact developed a human poverty index but uses it only for developing countries; according to this index Turkey is ranked twenty-fourth among 124 developing nations. For worldwide comparisons, we have only the HDI and its accompanying quality of life indicators. Petras and Veltmeyer criticize these indicators for their lack of context and argue that they create an illusion of success by hiding the costs associated with these material achievements: "Looking only at quality of life indicators only provides us with a concise and transient 'photography' of development, rather than a larger and long-term understanding of the trajectory of development and its structural roots" (2001, 124).

Turkey's record in human development ranks near the middle, eighty-fifth on a list of 174 countries. Table 5.3 lists selected human development and quality of life indicators, as well as average OECD statistics to provide a comparative framework. Even though Turkey has made significant progress in the last few decades, it still lags behind the OECD average as far as health, mortality, and gender-related indicators. Turkey's gender-related development index (GDI), which measures the "disparity in achievement between women and men" (UNDP 2000, 270), is lower than its HDI, implying that men's education, income, and life expectancy exceed those of women. Indeed, the female literacy rate is 81 percent of that for men and the women's economic activity rate is 59.4 percent of the men's. The increase in participation by women has directly resulted from urbanization, which helped transform the extended family structure into a nuclear family structure. The participation rate has been limited, however, by the lack of an infrastructure to support working women, for example, affordable child-care centers. The remaining data in Table 5.3 indicate that durable goods consumption is rising, that Turks have a protein- and fat-rich diet, and that Turkey is catching up with the rest of the OECD. However, the consumption-oriented quality of life indicators invite a healthy dose of skepticism. According to Table 5.3, 286 people out of 1,000 own a TV set in Turkey, but another interpretation would argue that 714 out of 1,000 are deprived of TV and have not benefited from Turkey's consumption-led growth and development.

What has Turkey gained from economic liberalization and at what cost? Definitely the benefits of liberalization have accrued disproportionately to the economic elite, which established itself in the 1960s and 1970s under the import-substitution policies and then showed the flexibility to switch to exports. Those companies unable to make this switch disappeared. Another group of winners were newcomers to the export and financial sectors, the nouveau riche. A third group of winners were the managers, especially high- and mid-level managers, well-educated, young, and ambitious, who have been the key factor behind Turkey's economic growth. It is ironic that economic liberalization based on export promotion and privatization depends so much on import-substitution and the public sector. The industrial base upon

Table 5.3. Selected Human Development Indicators, 1998

Health and Mortality
Human Development Index (HDI)

Life Expectancy at Birth	OECD	0.893	
	Turkey	0.732	

		1970–75	1995–2000
Infant Mortality Rate (per 1000 live births)			
	OECD	74	81
	Turkey	67	72

		1970	1998
Doctors per 100,000 people (1992–95)			
	OECD	15	6
	Turkey	133	42
	OECD	222	
	Turkey	103	

Gender Equality

Gender-Related Development Index (GDI) (1998)	OECD	0.889	
	Turkey	0.726	

Female Adult Literacy (as % of male rate, 1998)	OECD	n/a	
	Turkey	81	

Female Economic Activity Rate (as % of male rate, 1998)	OECD	69.3	
	Turkey	59.4	

		1990	1996–98
Consumer Goods Televisions per 1000 people	OECD	531	621
	Turkey	230	286

Nutritional Needs

		1970	1997
Daily Per Capita Supply of Calories			
	OECD	3033	3380
	Turkey	3053	3525

		1970	1997
Daily Per Capita Supply of Fat			
	OECD	102.2	125
	Turkey	62.3	101

		1990	1996–98
Personal Computers per 1000 people			
	OECD	94	255
	Turkey	5	23

		1970	1997
Daily Per Capita Supply of Protein			
	OECD	88.6	101
	Turkey	90.8	98

Source: World Bank, 2000.

which export promotion relies arose in the import-substitution era. Privatization targets public sector activity that private capital once regarded as unprofitable. An interesting feature of the Turkish case is the position of the military in this process. The military over the years emerged as an active player in the Turkish economy, a significant partner with the private sector in producing several consumer goods, such as motor vehicles. Hence, the military directly participates in production, appropriation, and distribution decisions in the economy. In the post-1980 liberalization and globalization era, it managed to maintain its political and economic power and to preserve its assets by strengthening that public-private partnership.

Liberalization has had a disproportionately adverse effect on the working class. Turkish labor has been the primary victim, not only in loss of wages, but also, more importantly, in loss of rights. The 1982 Constitution effectively eliminated all the rights of the workers. A new law in 1997 revived unions' right to participate in political life in a limited way, but unionization had already dropped to 14 percent over the fifteen years between 1982 and 1997 (Kongar 1999, 630). The current constitution still limits the freedom to strike, requiring prior collective bargaining and mediation, and prohibiting strikes by certain groups of workers and civil servants. Nevertheless, there are currently over thirty trade unions and the right to organize and bargain collectively is expanding. In addition to the working class, elderly, and unemployed young, another group that became worse off in the post-1980 period was the bureaucracy. Privatization not only transferred wealth from public to private sectors, but also led to a transfer of economic and political power from the state bureaucracy to the private sector, domestic and foreign. An immediate consequence of such a transfer is that the state loses its traditional grip on certain economic sectors, which once promoted industries strategic for national security or that no longer attract the long-term, large-scale, private investment needed for a viable production and distribution infrastructure. Petras and Veltmeyer refer to the latter: "Without the huge push from the public sector to establish basic infrastructure and industry, state financing and contracts, it is hard to imagine where today's free markets would be" (2001, 95).

In spite of the fact that liberalization and globalization has instituted its own economic, political, and social power relationships, proponents of liberalization would argue that one of its most important gains has been the infusion of democracy. In the next section we look briefly at the relationships between economic liberalization and political and economic democracy.

LIBERALIZATION AND DEMOCRACY

In the last two decades, political democracy has replaced most military dictatorships in developing countries, especially in Latin America. Political democracy has not, however, been accompanied by economic democracy. As the private sector, multinationals, and international bank and nonbank financial institutions accumulated profits (and as poverty and income inequality consequently increased), economic freedom—the freedom to participate in the market and make decisions about what, how, and for whom to produce—decreased. Wealth and income concentration meant the concentration of power in the hands of the economic elite. Thus liberalization created class relations in developing countries that left them far from democratic.

The relationship among economic liberalization, political liberalization, and economic democracy demonstrates that economic liberalization does not automatically lead to political liberalization and economic democracy. In the West, it took a long time for today's individual liberties to emerge. Three developments played a crucial role. First, nation-states were established, engendering an immense movement of people, capital, and wealth into the urban centers, where the political, social, economic, and cultural lives of the nation-states became centered. This concentration of the population led to a rising urban bourgeoisie, which acquired significant power and asserted its liberties against the sovereign. Second, in the sixteenth and seventeenth centuries, the arrival of precious metals from America, as well as growth of a banking system, resulted in the creation of an effective market economy. Third, Renaissance philosophy and Reformation theology placed the individual at the center. The Renaissance brought respect for the human being as an individual and the Reformation laid the basis for freedom of conscience. In the seventeenth century, beginning with Descartes, a whole philosophical system based on individual thought flourished. The Enlightenment opened a new era of modernity, one of whose most significant elements was the individuation process, the transformation of human beings into autonomous individuals. Particularly from the nineteenth century on, this process took a new turn. Economic, social, and political changes brought new patterns, new paradigms, to the thinking and behavior of citizens in industrial societies. The individual progressively grew emancipated from religious, family, and communitarian ties, making choices freely and assuming sole responsibility for those choices. In the development of the Western concept of individual liberties, the individual provided the basis of the value system that in turn provided the foundation of the political and judicial systems. This individuation process led to the flourishing of the market system and political democracy.

Historically, one could argue, economic liberalization has inspired the instituting of fundamental human rights and political liberalization and democracy. The rise of the middle classes, along with their demand to share political and economic power, has driven the political liberalization process. Contemporary examples of economic liberalization's role in leading to political liberalization abound in countries that experimented with IMF/World Bank-sponsored liberalization programs. Political liberalization has remodeled developing countries' social, political, and economic institutions after their Western counterparts by establishing and defending first the rights protecting private property, and then basic human freedoms, especially the right to live free of state repression. This is all fine and should be supported. However, economic and political liberalization does not necessarily bring economic democracy. In economic democracy, workers participate in decision making in production, appropriation, and distribution. One could argue that contemporary economic and political liberalization have progressed at the expense of economic democracy by systematically favoring global capital and marginalizing labor.

The evolution of human rights in Turkey is a classic example of how capital-driven economic liberalization promotes political liberalization and democracy, and even basic individual rights, but intentionally fails to recognize economic democracy. The discourse regarding political and human rights in Turkey has always focused on Westernization and, consequently, on the ethical values of the Enlightenment. Economic democracy has never been a concern. Recent reforms dictated by the European Union call for the establishment of institutions that would comfort global capital, increase its profitability, and strengthen the institutions that support private property rights. Therefore, democratization in Turkey has been confined to the political sphere.

In the early 1980s Özal's economic reforms and policies aimed at opening up the economy to the outside world and establishing a market system. In other words, one of its main objectives was to diminish the state's role and increase the private sector's. Hence, Özal's reforms were basically economic, not intended to cover political or individual rights. The Constitution and laws of the military regime of 12 September 1981 had curtailed fundamental rights and freedoms, especially those of the working class. This erosion of labor rights since 1980 has been a defining characteristic of the Turkish liberalization. Post-1980 liberalization and privatization policies and decreasing union power in Turkey have similarly contributed to a worsening income inequality. The fact that Turkish labor unions have for almost two decades been excluded from participation in economic and political life has severely limited democratization. Turkish authorities since 1980 have continuously regarded labor as a barrier to successful economic liberalization. The suppression of labor and the new flexible labor market have created the desired liberal environment for domestic and international capital to enjoy high profits. One could have expected that Özal, after coming to power with a comfortable majority, would also liberalize Turkey politically. Such hopes were not realized, partly because Özal believed he could implement his economic reforms more comfortably and effectively in a regulated political environment. After all, the restrictions on individual liberties of the 12 September regime were not his own making, and Özal himself was a conservative politician.

Liberalization, on the other hand, led to the emergence of a new class of wealthy entrepreneurs. This new generation of businessmen was well-educated, modern, and outward-looking, and Özal nurtured a new relationship between the State and business circles. Until Özal's coming to power in 1983, the import-substitution policies required the close dependency of industrialists upon the government. With Özal's export-oriented free market policies, this relationship changed drastically. The state no longer regulated economic forces and gave every support to businesses. Successful business managers from the private sector filled key positions in the administration. In such an environment, private enterprise flourished. The Turkish business community's contacts with the outside world increased greatly as they established close relations with multinationals and explored foreign markets (Ilkin 1991, 193–98). All these changes made the new entrepreneur class in Turkey powerful and assertive in setting priorities and formulating policies, becoming an influential force in the modernization and democratization of Turkey. Business elite's active support for joining the European Union was not motivated by economic interest alone: they saw membership as an opportunity to raise the standards of democracy and human rights to the European level.

The efforts of big business to democratize Turkey became particularly effective within TÜSIAD (Turkish Industrialists' and Businessmen's Association). TÜSIAD as a pressure group has proved instrumental in giving the business community a political voice. TÜSIAD, which defines itself as a liberal, democratic, pro-Western association, expresses its views on economic, political matters through press conferences and publications. For instance, a report prepared under its auspices defines the primary political criteria that would strengthen political democracy in Turkey and ease its acceptance into the European Union as freedom of expression, freedom of association and peaceful assembly, freedom from torture, and the maintenance of the de facto moratorium on capital punishment (TÜSIAD 2001, 10). TÜSIAD's active interest in human rights and democracy in Turkey is not an abstract concern but is closely related to economic interests of the business community. TÜSIAD representatives have openly stated that if Turkey does not improve its human rights record, Turkish businesses might lose their commercial relations with Europe, with dreadful economic consequences for the country.

The overlapping of business interests with democracy and human rights is not unique to Turkey and occurs throughout Western history. However, two major differences exist in the case of Turkey. First, in the West, individual liberties were asserted against the state. The acceptance of human rights as a value system resulted from conflicts between the State and the bourgeoisie. In Turkey, demand for human rights and democracy has never incited a confrontation between the State and business community. The new entrepreneur class has always been cautious about not losing state support. Second, the market economy and industrialization in the West created a strong middle class that was the prime beneficiary and supporter of human rights. In Turkey, Özal's economic policies, particularly the high rates of inflation and unemployment that became permanent elements of the Turkish economy, destroyed the existing middle and working classes, increasing poverty and inequality. This increased economic disparity led to a decrease in tax revenues. Consequently, funds allocated to health, education, and unemployment benefits were rendered inadequate. Such economic and social conditions created a hostile climate for the development of human rights.

In the 1980s, Özal's economic reforms and policies integrated the Islamic business circles, which until then had remained at the periphery, into the economy. At the beginning this process moved slowly, but the pace of integration increased, leading to a substantial accumulation of Islamic capital. A new bourgeoisie arose in Turkey, consisting of employers and employees of middle-sized companies as well as traditional Anatolian tradesmen. The important feature of this new middle class is that it exists outside the traditional secular business elite and thus is not dominated by its ideas or reflexes. This new Islamic bourgeoisie played an important political role by becoming the main financial source of Islamic political parties. Necmettin Erbakan's Welfare Party (Refah Partisi) and its successor, Virtue Party (Fazilet Partisi), both now dissolved, always had close links with Islamic capital. As a result of the financial assistance it provided the Islamic bourgeoisie gained significant political power.

The new Islamic Justice and Development Party (AKP) that came to power with a landslide victory in the November 2002 elections drew support mainly from this new middle class and Islamic big business. It endorses a Turkish bourgeois ideology that synthesizes religion and capitalism, not very differently from ideologies of Western European political parties like Christian Democrats. A political party of this character is bound to be guided by the requirements of a modern society in its economic platform as well as its stand on political liberties. In fact, the Justice and Development Party sees Turkey's membership in the European Union as one of its main targets and has committed itself to radical reforms in human rights in addition to economic policy initiatives. Thus, the political and economic elite have, for different reasons, regarded the political and economic liberalization of the Turkish economy as a fundamental reform in the quest for EU membership. The modernization-cum-liberalization strategy would create an economic environment attractive to European financial capital, and without a strong working class, the accompanying political and social freedom would supplement the economic reforms. The wishes of domestic and international capital would thus come true, while social and political freedoms would also enable certain nonsecular, religious groups to carry out their agendas without fear of backlash from the army.

Political freedom is the first necessary step toward including the economically disadvantaged in the political sphere, where they would have a vote and a voice. Political freedom would inevitably have positive linkages to economic and social freedoms and rights. But political freedom without a more equal distribution of income and wealth would not succeed in providing complete individual freedom. Economic freedom, reflected in economic equality and in participation in economic decision making, is necessary to enhance individual capabilities and freedoms (Sen 1999). In this sense, democratization in Turkey could be a step in the right direction, although a seriously limited one.

To conclude, a free market may be necessary for the expansion of democracy and human rights. The mere existence of a free market creates new dynamics, and in the Turkish case, the dynamics of the post–1980 period created a new bourgeoisie, partly secular and partly religious, and, with its strong support, Turkey's efforts to integrate with Europe. But even if the free market is a necessary condition for political democracy, human rights, and EU membership, it is not sufficient by itself to establish a liberal democratic society built on the principles of economic democracy, equity, and fairness.

Global Capital and International Labor

Economic liberalization is an extension of neoliberalism, an ideology based on a relationship between capital and labor that reinforces the concentration of wealth and income in the hands of the economic elite. An alternative within the same framework would redefine the relationship between capital and labor.

The neoliberal emphasis on capital and wealth accumulation derives from income and welfare maximization approaches to economic development. However, economic development is more than growth in per capita income. It incorporates income growth but also emphasizes equal distribution of income and environmental sustainability. The Turkish experience with liberalization has achieved some income growth but has certainly failed in distributing gains equally and in avoiding environmental degradation. Amartya Sen, the winner of the 1998 Nobel Prize in Economics, introduces a new paradigm in his *Development as Freedom* (1999) by defining development as a process of removing what he calls individual "unfreedoms" and expanding substantive freedoms. This paradigm operates on a freedoms-functionings-capabilities axis so that eliminating existing unfreedoms—for instance, poverty, tyranny, and barriers to social, economic, and political opportunities—while expanding human rights, reinforces the functionings of an individual, where functionings are conditions an individual values. Freedom to achieve a full set of functionings leads to enhanced capabilities and helps the individual choose a life "one has reason to value" (Sen 1999, 74). Thus, Sen's capabilities approach focuses on providing individuals the ability to pursue their own lives as they see fit. The emphasis on individual opportunities, rights, entitlements, and freedoms frees the development paradigm from the income and welfare dicta of traditional, neoclassical economic theory and elevates it to a higher plateau where freedom and equality count. According to Sen, capital and wealth accumulation is only a means to achieve true development and not an end in itself. Health, employment, education, environmental sustainability, and political participation become equally important conditions. Note that for Sen, equality is not limited to equal distribution of income. His concept of the equality of capabilities focuses on substantive freedoms that allow people to achieve the functionings they value. Within this context labor rights are an integral part of fundamental human rights and part of a "decent society" (Sen 2000, 123). Mishra (2001) further argues that labor rights should be treated as human rights if we desire a productive, motivated, and stable labor force. Guaranteeing these rights will ensure that economic progress will proceed hand in hand with social and economic equity (Mishra 2001, 13).

Sen's primary concern is distributive justice. He argues that people with greater needs be provided more resources in order to attain the same level of capabilities as those who are better endowed. Sen recognizes the need for several social, economic, and political institutions to provide, enhance, and equalize capabilities. The market provides economic opportunities and freedoms, the state provides the basic needs and the necessary public policy, and democratic institutions safeguard civil rights and political freedoms to enhance overall freedom and capabilities.

It is extremely hard for an individual to realize capabilities without the support of an institutional framework that can enhance the functionings and capabilities of groups of people. Nongovernmental organizations (NGOs), such as Greenpeace, are examples of how such organizations can provide the necessary institutional support in expanding capabilities. Similarly, revitalizing labor organizations would provide the necessary institutional framework to help labor expand its capabilities. A working class that is unionized and well organized would help workers shed the "unfreedoms" imposed on them by global capital in the last two decades or so. Labor market flexibility has cost labor its power to organize effectively and to challenge global capital. Dwindling unionization rates, cuts in social welfare provisions, and the loss of its traditional weight in politics, especially in Western industrialized countries, have marginalized labor and minimized its capabilities. Strengthening the labor movement at the global level would, to some extent, rid labor of the unfreedoms it has experienced during the last two decades and hence raise its capabilities to achieve equal footing with global capital. Membership in a "Fordist" consumer society that encourages the accumulation of significant personal debt has effectively neutralized workers in industrial counties such as the United States. These workers are more concerned with the payment of debt than with their work conditions and, more importantly, their exploitation. In the developing world, workers are, at least so far, more politically engaged and more aware of the extent of their exploitation by international financial capital. In Brazil, for instance, Luiz Inacio Lula daSilva won the elections in 2002 because of labor's support. In February 2001, workers in Turkey (as in Argentina and elsewhere in Asia, Africa, and Latin America) took to the streets protesting the IMF and its liberalization program. The anger and the energy are there; labor needs to capitalize on them. Labor movements in semiperiphery countries like Turkey can provide the necessary leadership for international labor movements. As Boswell (2000) argues, in the periphery, there is motivation but no opportunity, while labor in most core countries suffers from lack of motivation. In the semiperiphery countries, both motivation and opportunity exist, since these countries are more industrialized and hence their workers are more conscious of their class identity and exploitation. Eventually they could lead the international mobilization of labor.

It is a good time to renegotiate the relationship between capital and labor, in Turkey and elsewhere. Global capital is currently in crisis. The instability of capital markets in the first half of 2002, corporate scandals, dwindling profits, and increasing criticisms of globalization, liberalization, the IMF, and the World Bank have deepened this crisis. Workers' rights, such as unionization, pensions, working hours, working conditions, and wages, need to be reevaluated. Democratic labor unions should be politically reorganized. Developing countries are not strong enough to stand up individually against global capital; workers in developing countries as well as in industrial countries need to act together to gain power. Cross-border labor organizing is the only effective way of containing global capital's power.

Reenergizing the labor movement at a global level, revitalizing labor unions, renewing the participation of labor in political life, and restructuring work conditions are necessary aspects of a new relationship between capital and labor. They are not, however, sufficient. Global capital uses international organizations such as the IMF, World Bank, and WTO to impose its will on developing countries. Democratization of these organizations would be a concomitant part of global restructuring. Developing countries, as sovereign nation states, should have equal footing with industrial countries in the decision-making process at these institutions.

Of course, global capital would resist such a loss of profits and power, so the nation state needs to redefine itself into a catalyst for this change. In the last two decades, global capital has formed a successful partnership with nation-states in the developing world and has penetrated their economies. The "third way" provided the intellectual foundation for the new role of the state, and privatization facilitated its implementation. As a result, nation-states lost their sovereignty and assumed a subordinate position in the core-periphery hierarchy, strengthening the grip of global capital. The sovereign nation state must reestablish itself in all venues of life, but especially in the economy, as the producer of strategic goods like energy and, equally important, as the overseer of the rights of its workers and its people. If the nation state is strong and supports its workers and its people, global capital will have no choice but to accept labor as an equal partner.

A possible productive reorganization of the relationship between labor and capital within the context of contemporary neoliberalism is proposed in Figure 5.2. The figure supplements Figure 5.1 by allowing labor-led initiatives (the right-hand-side boxes) to balance the current hegemony of capital. The main aim of the proposed scheme is to allow the working classes the opportunity to realize their freedoms, functionings, and capabilities, as argued by Sen, by strengthening the trade unions and other labor organizations. Without the latter, the working classes would lack the necessary institutional framework to help them realize their goals. A strong and democratic trade union movement in the core, as well as in the semiperiphery and periphery, is essential for the success of the global labor movement, and it can only be achieved with the support of sovereign na-

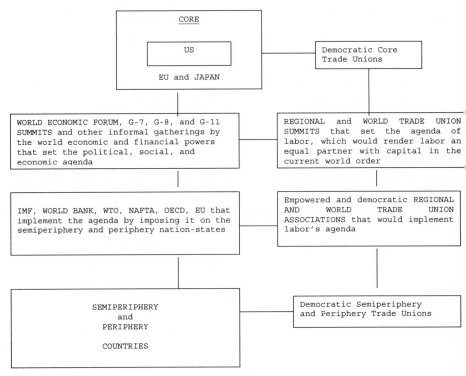

Figure 5.2. The Modified Core-Periphery Model

tion-states. The organization of international trade union associations and trade union summits, on the other hand, would bring labor into the global decision-making mechanism regarding the social, political, and economic power relationships between labor and capital, providing necessary checks and balances. These new initiatives would change the relationship between the core and the semiperipheral and peripheral countries significantly. The empowerment of the working class at a global level would enable it to negotiate effectively with global capital regarding the production, appropriation, and distribution of the economic surplus in the core as well as in the periphery and semiperiphery.

The International Labor Organization (ILO) has recently been active in organizing labor to limit the control of the world economy by global capital. The ILO initiated the Copenhagen World Summit in 1995 and the 1998 International Labor Conference. The 1998 Declaration on the Fundamental Principles and Rights at Work promoted labor rights, social protection, and cooperation among trade unions. The Declaration (the full text of the declaration can be accessed at the ILO Web page http://www.ilo.org/) elaborates in detail the following core principles regarding labor: freedom of association, the right to collective bargaining, and the elimination of slave labor. Unfortunately, the ILO has no enforcement power to make sure that these principles are actually applied, so one way of empowering the ILO would be to incorporate it into the decision-making mechanisms of the IMF, the World Bank, and WTO. The ILO's full and direct participation at these organizations would enable it to represent labor concerns and rights effectively.

The empowerment of the ILO is a necessary but not a sufficient condition for the success of the new labor movement. The nation-state and national labor organizations also need restructuring and reorientation. As Gindin (2000) points out, neoliberalism is a class movement that has created a global economy, the rules of which are set by global business. Traditionally these rules have been set by nation-states on the basis of an existing social contract (Faux 2004), reflecting unwritten social norms and values that include local culture and traditions. The social contract complements the written laws, shaping the relationship between capital and labor, between the state and capital labor, and between the state and the citizens. Globalization, however, has dismantled the existing social contracts and has removed the interests of international financial capital from the nation-states' control. The reemergence of the democratic and strong nation-state defining and protecting the core freedoms and rights of its citizens and of labor is a fundamental requirement for the alternative strategy to become successful. The nation-state, after all, can structure social relations so labor, left out of social discourse for more than two decades, is once again included. The national trade unions also need to be strengthened by enlarging their membership base and becoming more democratic and open. The traditional male domination of trade unions does not reflect the increasing participation of women and migrant workers in the labor force. The democratization of trade unions will allow these new groups their proper voice in the organized labor movement. Trade unions also need to be open to new internationalism and international solidarity, and thus willing to argue for the inclusion of labor rights in international trade and financial agreements (Tabb 2002). This new international orientation will facilitate the formation of effective international trade unions and summits as described in Figure 5.2.

As we already have mentioned, after a two-decade-long dormancy Turkish trade unions are once again forming and workers are awakening. This revival of the trade union movement is essential for the Turkish workers to realize their full capabilities and freedoms and for the establishment of full economic democracy in Turkey. The Turkish trade unions, especially DISK (the Confederation of Progressive Trade Unions) and TURK-Is (the Turkish Confederation of Workers' Unions) have a long history in the political and economic life of the country. They could assume a leadership position in the domestic, as well as international, labor movement by reviving themselves and emphasizing social movement unionism, economic equality, democratization, and international solidarity.

Global capital imposed liberalization with the dictum "there is no alternative." Nation states and labor, once they have redefined, revitalized, and restructured themselves, should impose equal partnership on global capital with the identical dictum: "There is no alternative."

Appendices

APPENDIX 1.A: PER CAPITA INCOME GROWTH AND POLICY TARGET VARIABLES

The OLS estimate of the model for 1980–2000 is (t-statistics in parenthesis):

$$Ygr = 1.082E\text{-}02 - .175CRIS^* - 2.431E\text{-}03INF^* + .718BSR + 7.095E\text{-}04OP^{**}$$
$$(.107) \quad (-2.524) \quad (-2.268) \quad (.599) \quad (1.877)$$

adjusted $R^2 = .349$
$N = 21$

where,

Ygr: per capita GNP growth
CRIS: crisis dummy, takes on 1 in crisis years
INF: CPI inflation
BSR: budget surplus-GNP ratio
OP: openness measured as (exports+imports)/GNP

Data is from SIS, various issues.

* significant at five percent
** significant at ten percent

APPENDIX 2.A: THE ACCELERATOR MODEL OF MANUFACTURING INVESTMENT

The accelerator model of manufacturing used in this study assumes that investment, I, by the manufacturing firms responds to the changes in the current and lagged sales, ΔS and ΔS_{-1}, and in profits, $\Delta \pi$, as internal sources of finance,

$$I = f(\Delta S, \Delta S(-1), \Delta \pi)$$

A modified version of this model is tested here that incorporates the real interest rate, i, and the volume of transactions in the stock market, *FIN*, and a time trend, *T*:

$$I = f(\Delta S, \Delta S(-1), \Delta \pi, i, FIN, T)$$

The investment, sales, and profit data used in the estimation are for the five hundred largest manufacturing firms in Turkey as compiled by the Istanbul Chamber of Industry. It covers ten years, from 1986 to 1998. Interest rate and stock market data are from IMF, International Financial Statistics (2001), and Istanbul Stock Exchange (2002), respectively. The nominal interest rate is adjusted for CPI inflation to calculate the real interest rate. The CPI data is also from the IMF. The sample size in the pooled regression analysis is 1,923. The model assumes that firms are affected identically by the two macroeconomic variables, the interest rate and stock market transactions. The result is presented below (** is significant at 5%, * at 10%):

$I = 11.20 + .38^* \Delta S + 3.15^{**} \Delta S_{-1} + .70^* \Delta \pi + .13^{**} T + 3.16^* E\text{-}03i - 3.12E\text{-}06 \text{ FIN}$
    (1.39)   (2.51)   (18.95)   (1.19)   (14.61)   (2.58)   (−.50)

adj. $R^2 = .40$
    $N = 1923$

Bibliography

Acker, D. 1989. Food Aid Programs. *1988 World Food Conference Proceedings*, 161–66. Ames, Iowa: ISUP for the Center for Agricultural and Rural Development.

Akcay, C., E. Alper, and M. Karasulu. 1997. Currency Substitution and Exchange Rate Instability: The Turkish Case. *European Economic Review* 41 (3): 827–35.

Akyuz, Y. 1990. Financial System and Policies in Turkey in the 1980s. In *The Political Economy of Turkey: Debt, Adjustment and Sustainability*, eds. T. Aricanli and D. Rodrik. New York: MacMillan.

Albo, G. 2002. Neoliberalism, the State, and the Left: A Canadian Perspective. *Monthly Review* 54 (1): 46–55.

Amin, S. 1976. *Imperialism and Unequal Development*. New York: Monthly Review Press.

Anand, R., and S. Wijnbergen. 1988. *Inflation, External Debt and Financial Sector Reform: A Quantitative Approach to Consistent Fiscal Policy with an Application to Turkey*. NBER Working Paper No. 2731. Washington, DC: NBER.

Aricanli, T., and D. Rodrik. 1999. An Overview of Turkey's Experience with Economic Liberalization and Structural Adjustment. In *The Political Economy of the Middle East*. Elgar Reference Collection, Vol. 4. Cheltenham, England: Elgar Publishers.

Aricanli, T., and D. Rodrik, eds. 1990. *The Political Economy of Turkey*. New York: St. Martin's Press.

Athey, M., and P. Laumas. 1994. Internal Funds and Corporate Investment in India. *Journal of Development Economics* 45:287–303.

Atiyas, I. 1990. The Private Sectors Response to Liberalization in Turkey: 1980–82. In *The Political Economy of Turkey*, ed. T. Aricanli and D. Rodrik. New York: St. Martin's Press.

Bailey, P. 2000. *Is There a Decent Way to Break Up Ships?* Geneva, Switzerland: International Labor Organization.

Balassa, B. 1989. Outward Orientation. In *Handbook of Development Economics*, Vol. 2, ed. H. Chenery and T. N. Srinivasan. Amsterdam, Holland: Elsevier Science Publishers.

———. 1978. Exports and Economic Growth: Further Evidence. *Journal of Development Economics* 5 (2): 181–89.

Bank of International Settlements. 1997. *Financial Stability in Emerging Market Economies*. Basel: Bank for International Settlements.

Barajas, A., R. Steiner, and N. Salazar. 2000. The Impact of Liberalization and Foreign Investment in the Colombian Financial Sector. *Journal of Development Economics* 63 (1): 157–96.

Barkan, J. 2000. The Third Way/Die Neue Mitte: A Manifesto. *Dissent* (April): 51–65.

Barkin, D. 1987. The End of the Food Self-Sufficiency in Mexico. *Latin American Perspectives* 14 (3): 271–97.

———. 1983. The Internationalization of Capital and the Spatial Organization of Agriculture in Mexico. In *Regional Analysis and the International Division of Labor*, ed. F. Moulaert and P. W. Salinas. Boston: Kluwer-Nijhoff.

Basel Convention the Control of Transboundary Movements of Hazardous Wastes and Their Disposal. 1989. Geneva: Secreteriat of the Basel Convention.

Bentley, J. 1997. Shapes of world history in twentieth-century scholarship. Unpublished.

Birdsall, N., and D. Wheeler. 1993. Trade Policy and Industrial Pollution in Latin America. Where Are the Pollution Havens? *Journal of Environment and Development* 2 (1): 137–49.

Boeke, J. H. 1953. *Economics and Economic Policy in Dual Societies.* New York: AMS Press.

Boswell, T. 2000. *The Spirit of Capitalism and Socialism: Toward Global Democracy.* Boulder, Co: Lynne Rienner Publishers, Inc.

Bosworth, B., and S. Collins. 1999. Capital Flows to Developing Economies: Implications for Saving and Investment. *Brookings Papers on Economic Activity* (1) : 143–80.

Brecker, R., and E. Choudhri. 1994. Pareto Gains From Trade Reconsidered: Compensation for Jobs Lost. *Journal of International Economics* 36 (3–4): 223–38.

Bryceson, D. 1997. An Agrarian Continent in Transition. *Africa Now: People, Policies, and Institutions.* London: Currey.

Cakmak, E. 1998. Agricultural policy reforms and rural development in Turkey. Paper presented at the Mediterranean Development Forum. Marrakech.

Cakmak, E., et al. 1996. The Rural Economy Under Structural Adjustment and Financial Liberalization. *Canadian Journal of Development Studies* 17 (3): 427–47.

Celasun, O., C. Denizer, and D. He. 1997. Capital flows, macroeconomic management, and the financial system: The Turkish case, 1989–97. Unpublished Paper.

Chase-Dunn, C. 1996. World Systems: Similarities and Differences. In *Essays in Honor of Andre Gunder Frank: The Underdevelopment of Development*, ed. S. Chew and R. Denemark. 246–57. London: Sage Publications, Inc.

Claassens, S., A. Demirguc-Kunt, and H. Huizinge. 1998. *How Does Foreign Entry Affect the Domestic Banking Market?* World Bank Policy Resarch Working Paper No. 1918. Washington, DC: World Bank.

Cochrane, W., and F. Runge. 1992. *Reforming Farm Policy: Towards a National Agenda.* Ames: Iowa State University Press.

Cole, M. 2000. *Trade Liberalization, Economic Growth and the Environment.* Northampton, MA: Edward Elgar.

Conway, P. 1994. IMF Lending Programs: Participation and Impact. *Journal of Development Economics* 45 (2): 365–91.

Dasgupta, P., and K. Maler. 1995. Poverty, Institutions and the Environmental Resource Base. In *Handbook of Development Economics,* ed. J. Behrmand and T. N. Srinivasan. Amsterdam: Elsevier Science B.V.

David, B. et al. 2000. The Impact of the New Economic Model on Latin America'a Agriculture. *World Development* 28 (9): 1673–88.

Davis, J. et al. 2000. Fiscal and Macroeconomic Impact of Privatization. Occasional Paper No. 194. Washington, DC: The International Monetary Fund.

De Soto, H. 2000. *Mystery of Capital.* New York: Basic Books.

Dean, J. 1992. Trade and the Environment. World Bank Working Paper Series 966. Washington, DC: The World Bank.

Dervis, K., and P. Petri. 1987. The Macroeconomics of Successful Development: What are the Lessons? In *NBER Macroeconomics Annual: 1987,* ed. S. Fischer. Cambridge: MIT Press.

Dollar, D. 1992. Outward Oriented Developing Economies Really Do Grow More Rapidly: Evidence From 95 LDCs, 1976–1985. *Economic Development and Cultural Change* 40 (3): 523–44.

Doroodian, K. 1993. Macroeconomic Performance and Adjustment under Policies Commonly Supported by the International Monetary Fund. *Economic Development and Cultural Change* 41 (4): 849–64.

Dos Santos, T. 1970. The Structure of Dependence. *American Economic Review* 60 (2): 2,312–36.

Economic Intelligence Unit (EIU). 1999. *Turkey.* London: The Economist.

Economic Report of the President. 2001. Washington, DC: US Government Printing Office.

Economist. 1995. Internal and External Funding of Investment (November), 80.

Edwards, S. 2001. *Capital Mobility and Economic Performance.* NBER Working Papers No. 8076. Washington, DC: National Bureau of Economic Research.

———. 1993. Openness, Trade Liberalization, and Growth in Developing Countries. *Journal of Economic Literature* 31 (3): 1, 358–93.

Ercel, G. 1999. Central Banking in Turkey. Unpublished speech at the Bulgarian National Bank, Sopia.

Esen, O. 2000. Financial Openness in Turkey. *International Review of Applied Economics* 14 (1): 4–23.

Essential Action. 2001. *Turkey-Privatization Implementation Assistance and Social Safety Net Project.* Staff Appraisal Report.

Eusufzai, Z. 1996. Openness, Economic Growth, and Development: Some Further Results. *Economic Development and Cultural Change* 44 (2): 333–38.

Faux, J. 2004. Without Consent: Global Capital Mobility and Democracy. *Dissent* (winter): 43–50.

Fazzari, S., R. Hubbard, and B. Petersen. 1988. Financial Constraints and Corporate Investment. *Brookings Papers on Economic Activity* (1):141–95.

Ferrantino, M., and L. Linkins. 1999. The Effect of Global Trade Liberalization on Toxic Emissions in Industry. *Weltwirtschaftliches Archiv* 135 (1): 128–55.

Ficici, A. 2000. Political economy of Turkish privatization: A critical assessment. Unpublished.

Folbre, N. 2001. *The Invisible Heart: Economics and Family Values.* New York: The New Press.

Forbes. 2002. The World's Billionaires (February 28).

Foster, J. B. 2002. Monopoly Capital and the New Globalization. *Monthly Review* 53 (8): 1–16.

Frank, A. G. 1966. *The Underdevelopment of Development.* New York: Monthly Review Press.

Friedman, T. 1999. *The Lexus and the Olive Tree: Understanding Globalization.* New York: First Anchor Books.

Friedmann, H. 1991. Changes in the International Division of Labor: Agri-Food Complexes and Export Agriculture, ed. In *Towards a New Political Economy of Agriculture.* H. Friedland et al., 65–93. Boulder, CO: Westview Press.

Fukuyama, F. 1991. *The End of History and the Last Man.* London: Hamish Hamilton.

Furman, J., and J. Stiglitz. 1998. Economic Crises: Evidence and Insights from East Asia. *Brookings Papers on Economic Activity* 2: 1–136.

Giddens, A. 2000. *The Third Way and its Critics.* Cambridge: Polity Press.

———. 1998. *The Third Way: The Renewal of Social Democracy.* Cambridge, UK: Polity Press.

Gindin, S. 2000. Turning Points and Starting Points: Brenner, Left Turbulence and Class Politics. In *Working Classes: Global Realities,* ed. L. Panitch and C. Lays, 342–66. London: The Merlin Press Ltd.

Gowan, P. 1999. *The Global Gamble: Washington's Faustian Bid for World Dominance.* London: Verso.

Grabel, I. 2002. Neoliberal Finance and Crisis in the Developing World. *Monthly Review* 53 (11): 34–46.

———. 1995. Speculation-Led Economic Development: A Post-Keynesian Interpretation of Financial Liberalization Programmes in the Third World. *International Review of Applied Economics* 9: 127–49.

Grossman, G. M., and A. M. Krueger. 1991. *Environmental Impact of a North American Free Trade Agreement.* NBER Working Paper 3914. Cambridge, MA: NBER.

Guncavdi, O., M. Bleaney, and A. McKay. 1998. Financial Liberalization and Private Investment: Evidence From Turkey. *Journal of Development Economics* 57 (2): 443–55.

Hardt, M., and A. Negri. 2000. *Empire.* Cambridge: Harvard University Press.

Henry, P. 2000. Do Stock Market Liberalizations Cause Investment Booms? *Journal of Financial Economics* 58 (1–2): 301–34.

Hirschman, A. 1958. *The Strategy of Economic Development.* New Haven: Yale University Press.

Hoekman, B., and K. Anderson. 2000. Developing-Country Agriculture and the New Trade Agenda. *Economic Development and Cultural Change* 49 (1): 171–80.

Huntington, S. 1996. *The Clash of Civilizations.* New York: Touchstone.

İlkin, S. 1991. Businessmen: Democratic Stability. In *Turkey and the West,* ed. M. Heper, A. Önur, and H. Kramer, 193–198. London: I.B. Tauris Publishers.

Inselbag, I., and B. Gultekin. 1988. Financial Markets in Turkey. In *Liberalization and the Turkish Economy,* ed. T. Nas and M. Odekon. Westport, CT: Greenwood Press.

International Energy Agency. 1999. *Energy Prices and Taxes*. Paris: International Energy Agency.

International Institute of Sustainable Development (IISP). 2000. *North American Symposium on Understanding the Linkages Between Trade and Environment*. Manitoba: International Institute of Sustainable Development.

International Monetary Fund (IMF). 2002. IMF Welcomes Turkey's Bank Recapitilization Scheme. *International Monetary Fund) News Brief* No. 02.

———. 2001a. *World Economic Outlook*. Washington, DC: IMF.

———. 2001b. *Turkey: Sixth and Seventh Reviews Under the Stand-By Arrangement. Staff Supplement and Press Release of the Executive Board*. Washington, DC: IMF.

———. 2001c. *Turkey: Eight Review Under the Stand-By Arrangement*. Washington, DC: IMF.

———. 2001d. *International Financial Statistics*. Yearbook 2001. Washington, DC: IMF.

———. 2000a. *Social Issues in IMF-Supported Programs*. Washington, DC: IMF.

———. 2000b. *Turkey: Selected Issues and Statistical Appendix*. Washington, D.C.: IMF.

Isaac, J. 2001. The Road (Not?) Taken. *Dissent* (April): 61–70.

Istanbul Chamber of Industry. *Turkey's 500 Major Industrial Enterprises*. Istanbul. Various issues.

Istanbul Stock Exchange. 2002. *Annual Factbook 2002*. Istanbul: Istanbul Stock Exchange.

Karatas, C. 1992. Privatization and Regulation in Turkey: An Assessment. *Journal of International Development* 4 (6): 583–605.

Keller, A. et al. 1994. Evaluating Privatization Policies in Turkey. *International Journal of Public Sector Management* 7 (1): 15–24.

Kepenek, Y., and N. Yenturk. 1994. *Turkiye Ekonomisi (Turkish Economy)*. Istanbul: Remzi Kitabevi.

Keyder, C. 1983. The Cycle of Sharecropping and the Consolidation of Small Peasant Ownership in Turkey. *Journal of Peasant Studies* 10 (1): 130–45.

Khan, M. 1990. *The Macroeconomic Effects of Fund-Supported Adjustment Programs*. IMF Staff Papers 37 (6): 195–231.

Khan, M., and M. Knight. 1985. *Fund-Supported Adjustment Programs and Economic Growth*. IMF Occasional Paper No. 41. Washington, DC: IMF.

Kjellstorm, S. 1990. *Privatization in Turkey*. World Bank Policy, Research, and External Affairs Working Paper No. 532. Washington, DC: World Bank.

Kongar, E. 1999. *21. Yuzyilda Turkiye (Turkey in the Twenty-first Century)*. Istanbul: Remzi Kitabevi.

Krueger, A. 1998. Whither the World Bank and the IMF? *Journal of Economic Literature* 36 (4): 1,983–2,020.

———. 1987. *The Importance of Economic Policy in Development: Contrasts between Korea and Turkey*. NBER Working Paper 2195. Cambridge, MA: NBER.

———. 1980. Trade Policy as an Input to Development. *American Economic Review* 70 (2): 288–92.

———, and O. Aktan. 1992. *Swimming Against the Tide: Turkish Trade Reform in the 1980s*. San Francisco: ICS Press.

Krugman, P. 1987. Is Free Trade Passe? *Economic Perspectives* 1 (2): 131–44.

Lane, S. 1995. The United States Food Policy. *American Journal of Agricultural Economics* 77 (5): 1,096–1,109.

Le Monde Diplomatique. 2002. L'Oppression du Developpement (September), 28.

Leibenstein, H. 1957. *Economic Backwardness and Economic Growth*. New York: Wiley.

Letters of Intent, 1989–2002, http://www.imf.org/external/country/TUR/index.htm?pn=0 and Memorandum on Economic Policies, 3 May 2001.

Low, P., and A. Yeats. 1992. *Do Dirty Industries Migrate?* World Bank Discussion Papers 159. Washington, DC: World Bank.

Lucas, R., D. Wheeler, and H. Hettige. 1992. *Economic Development, Environmental Regulation and the International Migration of Toxic Industrial Pollution 1960–88*. World Bank Policy Research Working Papers. Washington, DC: World Bank.

McMichael, P. 2000. Global Food Politics. In *Hungry for Profit*, ed. F. Magdoff et al. New York: Monthly Review Press.

———. 1996. *Development and Social Change: A Global Perspective*. Thousand Oaks, CA: Pine Forge Press.

Mesutoglu, B. 2001. *Turkiye'de Benzin Fiyatlarindaki Gelismeler, 1990–99* (Developments in Gasoline Prices in Turkey, 1990–99). Ankara: State Planning Organization.

Milliyet. 2000. *Buyuk Ihmal Olum Saciyor* (May 14).

Minsky, H. 1986. *Stabilizing an Unstable Economy*. New Haven: Yale University Press.

Mishra, L. 2001. Can Globalization and Labor Rights Coexist? *The Indian Journal of Labor Economics* 44 (1): 3–14.

Nas, T., and M. Odekon. 1998. Economic Liberalization and the Turkish Labor Market. In *Economic Liberalization and Labor Markets*. P. Dabir-Alai and M. Odekon, eds., 239–50. Westport, CT: Greenwood Press.

———. 1996. Effects of Post-1980 Macroeconomic Policies on Turkish Manufacturing. *Journal of Developing Areas* 30:211–22.

Nas, T., and M. Odekon, eds. 1992. *Economics and Politics of Turkish Liberalization*. Bethlehem, PA: Lehigh University Press.

———, eds. 1988. *Liberalization and the Turkish Economy*. Westport, CT: Greenwood Press.

National Environmental Action Plan of Turkey. 1999. Ankara: State Planning Organization.

New York Times. 2001. Move to Curb Biotech Crops Ignores Poor, UN Finds. July 8, 4.

New York Times Magazine. 2001. How Many Poor Children Is too Many? July 8, 3.

Nonneman, G. 1996. Economic Liberalization: The Debate. In *Political and Economic Liberalization: Dynamics and linkages in Comparative Perspective*, ed. G. Nonneman, London: Lynne Rienner Publishers, Inc.

Novak, M. 1998. *Is There a Third Way?* London: Institute of Economic Affairs Health and Welfare Unit.

Nurkse, R. 1953. *Problems of Capital Formation in Underdeveloped Countries*. New York: W.W. Norton and Company.

Odekon, M. 2003. *Foreign Investment in Turkey, 1980–2002*. Paper prepared for the

Fifty-eighth International Atlantic Economic Society Conference, Chicago, 7–10 October. Unpublished.

———. 1996. Liberalization and the environment in Turkey. Paper presented at the Eastern Economic Association Meeting, Boston, March. Unpublished.

———. 1988. Turkish Liberalization: From the Perspectives of Manufacturing Firms. In *Economics and Politics of Turkish Liberalization*, ed. T. Nas and M. Odekon, 155–75. Bethlehem, PA: Lehigh University Press.

———. 1988. Liberalization and the Turkish Economy. In *Liberalization and the Turkish Economy*, ed. T. Nas and M. Odekon, 29–46, Westport, CT: Greenwood Press.

OECD. *Economic Survey: Turkey*. Various issues.

———. 1999a. *Environmental Performance Reviews: Environmental Achievements in OECD Countries*. Paris: OECD.

Oyan, O. 2001. Tarimda Yapisal Uyarlama (Structural adjustment in agriculture). Unpublished.

Petras, J., and H. Veltmeyer. 2001. *Globalization Unmasked: Imperialism in the Twenty-first Century*. London: Zed Books.

———. 2000. The Third Way: Myth and Reality. *Monthly Review* 51 (10): 19–35.

———. 1979. *Critical Perspectives on Imperialism and Social Class*. New York: Monthly Review Press.

Pieper, U. and L. Taylor. 1998. The Revival of the Liberal Creed: The IMF, the World Bank, and Inequality in a Globalized Economy. In *Globalization and Progressive Economic Policy*, ed. D. Baker, et al. Cambridge: Cambridge University Press.

Polak, J. 1991. The changing nature of IMF conditionality. Technical Paper No. 41. Washington, DC: IMF.

Prebish, R. 1950. *The Economic Development of Latin America and Its Principal Problems*. New York: United Nations.

Reynolds, L., et al. 1993. The New Internationalization of Agriculture: A Reformulation. *World Development* 21 (7): 1,101–21.

Rigg, J., and S. Nattapoolwat. 2001. Embracing the Global in Thailand: Activism and Pragmatism in an Era of Deagrarianization. *World Development* 29 (6): 945–60.

Rodrik, D. 1999. *The New Global Economy and Developing Countries: Making Openness Work*. Washington, DC: Overseas Development Council.

———. 1997. *Has Globalization Gone Too Far?* Washington, DC: Institute for International Economics.

———. 1992. The Limits of Trade Policy Reform in Developing Countries. *Journal of Economic Perspectives* 6 (1): 87–105.

———. 1988. *Some Policy Dilemmas in Turkish Macroeconomic Management*. Discussion Paper Series No. 17SD. Cambridge: JFK School of Government, Harvard University.

Rosset, P. 2000. Cuba: A Successful Case Study of Sustainable Agriculture. In *Hungry for Profit*, ed. F. Magdoff, et al. New York: Monthly Review Press.

Rostow, W. 1960. *The Stages of Growth: A Non-Communist Manifesto*. London: Cambridge University Press.

Sanderson, S. 1985. The New Internationalization of Agriculture in Americas. In *The*

Americas in the New International Division of Labor, ed. S. Sanderson, 46–68. New York: Holmes and Meir.

Sarigedik, U. 2002. *Turkey: Grain and Feed Annual.* GAIN Report No. TU2014. Washington, DC: USDA.

Sayan, S. and A. Teksoz. 2001. Simulation Risks and Benefits from a Money Purchase Pension Scheme for Turkey. Paper presented at the Twenty-sixth Annual Meeting of the Middle East Economic Association. New Orleans, January 5–7.

Sen, A. 2000. Work and Rights. *International Labor Review* 139 (2): 119–28.

———. 1999. *Development as Freedom.* New York: Anchor Books.

Shafik, N., and S. Bandyopadhyay. 1992. *Economic Growth and Environmental Quality: Time Series and Cross-Country Evidence.* World Bank Policy Research Working Papers 904. Washington, DC: World Bank.

Shirreff, D. 1997. Tomorrow We Get Serious. *Euromoney* (November).

Singer, D. 1999. *Whose Millennium? Theirs or Ours?* New York: Monthly Review Press.

Sinha, R. 1995. Economic Reform in Developing Countries: Some Conceptual Issues. *World Development* 23 (4): 557–75.

Sirtioglu, I. 2002. *Turkey: HRI Food Service Sector.* GAIN Report No. TU2012. Washington, DC: USDA.

Somel, C. 2003. Estimating the Surplus in the Periphery: An Application to Turkey. *Cambridge Journal of Economics,* 17 (6): 919–33.

State Institute of Statistics (SIS). *Statistical Yearbook of Turkey.* Various issues.

State Planning Organization. 2002. *Main Economic Indicators.* Ankara: Devlet Planlama Mustasarligi.

Summers, L. 1991. Unpublished World Bank Memo (12 December).

Tabb, W. 2002. *Unequal Partners: A Primer on Globalization.* New York: The New Press.

Taylor, L. 1979. *Macro Models for Developing Countries.* New York: McGraw Hill.

T.C. Basbakanlik Hazine Dairesi. 1998. *Memorandum of Economic Policies.* Ankara: T.C. Basbakanlik Hazine Dairesi.

Thompson, S., and T. Cowan. 2000. Globalizing Agro-Food Systems in Asia: Introduction. *World Development* 28 (3): 401–407.

Tiller, A. 1996. *Orientation Notes: ACF Cuba Permaculture Program.* Fitzroy: Australian Conservation Foundation.

Tunali, Insan. 1993. Choice of Contracts in Turkish Agriculture. *Economic Development and Cultural Change* (January): 66–84.

Turk Kilavuz Kaptanlar Dernegi. 1999. *Turk Bogazlari Gecis ve Kaza Istatistikleri* (Turkish Maritime Pilots Associaiton. 1999. Turkish Straits passage and Casualty Statistics). Istanbul: TMPA.

TÜSIAD (Turkish Industrialists' and Businessmen's Association). 2001. *Perspectives on Democratization in Turkey and EU Copenhagen Political Criteria—Views and Priorities.* Publication No. t/2001–07/305. Istanbul: Lebib Yalkin Publishing and Printing Co.

Undersecreteriat of the Treasury. *Treasury Statistics.* Various issues. Ankara: Undersecreteriat of the Treasury.

United Nations Development Program (UNDP). 2000. *Human Development Report 2000.* New York: United Nations.

United Nations Environmental Program (UNEP). 2000. *Environment and Trade: A Handbook.* Winnipeg: UNEP.

United Nations. International Trade Statistics Yearbook. Various issues. New York: United Nations.

United Nations. 2002. *Report of the World Summit on Sustainable Development.* New York: United Nations.

U.S. Department of Agriculture. 2000. Turkey. *International Egg and Poultry Review.* 3 (33): 1

U.S. Department of Agriculture Economic Research Service. *FATUS, Commodities* (can be accessed at http://www.ers.usda.gov/data/fatus).

U.S. Energy Information Administration. 2002. *Turkey: Environmental Issues.* Washington, DC: United States Energy Information Administration.

Üstel, F. 2002. Türkiye Cumhmiyeti'nde Resmi Yurttaş Profilinin Evrimi (The Evolution of the Profile of Citizen in the Official Discourse in the Turkish Republic). In: *Milliyetçilik* (Nationalism). Istanbul: İletişim Yayınlar.

Valettee, J., and D. Wysham. 2002. *Enron's Pawns: How Public Institutions Bankrolled Enron's Globalization Game.* Washington, DC: Institute for Policy Studies.

Wallerstein, I. 1979. Dependence in an Interdependent World: The Limited Possibilities of Transformation Within the Capitalist World Economy, ed. In *The Capitalist World Economy.* I. Wallerstein. New York: Cambridge University Press.

———. 1975. The Present State of the Debate on World Inequality. In *World Inequality: Origins and Perspectives on the World System,* ed. I. Wallerstein. Montreal: Black Rose Books.

Weber, M. 1958. *The Protestant Ethic and the Spirit of Capitalism.* New York: Charles Scribner's Sons.

Wheeler, D., and P. Martin. 1993. National economic policy and industrial pollution. The case of Indonesia. 1975–89. Unpublished Paper. Washington, DC: World Bank.

Williamson, J. 1997. The Washington Consensus Revisited. In *Economic and Social Development into the Twenty-First Century,* ed. J. Williamson, 48–61. Washington, DC: Inter-American Development Bank.

Woodward, D. 1992. *Debt, Adjustment and Poverty in Developing Countries.* London: Pinter Publishers.

World Bank. 2001. *World Development Report 2001.* Washington, DC: World Bank.

———. 2000. *World Development Report 2000.* Washington, DC: World Bank.

———. 1995. *World Development Report 1995.* Washington, DC: World Bank.

———. 1992. *World Development Report 1992.* Washington, DC: World Bank.

———. 1991. *World Development Report 1991.* Washington, DC: World Bank.

———. 1990. *World Development Report 1990.* Washington, DC: World Bank.

World Resources Institute. 2001. *World Resources: A Guide to the Global Environment.* New York: Oxford University Press.

Xu, X., and L. Song. 2000. Regional Cooperation and the Environment: Do Dirty Industries Migrate? *Weltwirtschaftlicher Archiv* 136 (1): 137–57.

Yeldan, E. 1997. Financial Liberalization and Fiscal Repression in Turkey: Policy Analysis in a CGA Model with Financial Markets. *Journal of Policy Modeling* 19 (1): 79–117.

———, and G. Balkan. 1993. Industrialization, energy demand and environmental pollution under Turkish structural adjustment: A case study with implications for other countries. Unpublished.

Yenturk, N. 1997. The Last Fifteen Years of the Turkish Economy: Destined To Be in Crisis? *Private View* (autumn), 1–6.

Index